Department of Health and Social Security
Welsh Office

Report of the Working Party on Social Work Support for the Health Service

June 1974

LONDON
HER MAJESTY'S STATIONERY OFFICE
1974

SW—A

ISBN 0 11 320579 1

MEMBERSHIP OF THE WORKING PARTY

MR G J OTTON (Chairman)	Department of Health and Social Security
MR K A ABEL	Clerk, Dorset County Council
DR T H D ARIE	Consultant Psychiatrist, Goodmayes Hospital, Ilford
MISS H A BATE	Principal Social Worker, West Suffolk Hospital Management Committee
MR G C BATESON	Secretary, East Liverpool University Hospital Management Committee
MR W E BOYCE	Director of Social Services, Essex County Council
DR H O M BRYANT	Medical Officer of Health, West Bromwich County Borough
PROFESSOR A N EXTON-SMITH	Professor of Geriatric Medicine, University College Hospital
MR F E FOWLER	Director of Social Services, City of Westminster
MISS S M HALL	Principal Social Worker, Adolescent Department, Tavistock Clinic
MR V E JENKINS (resigned 7.11.73)	Director of Social Services, City of Cardiff
DR W G A RIDDLE	General Practitioner, Gateshead
DR P L ROBINSON	Consultant Physician, Clatterbridge Hospital, Cheshire
MR E B ROYCROFT	Director of Social Services, City of Newcastle
MISS P SERVICE	Principal Social Worker, Guy's Hospital
MR J H SMITH (appointed 7.11.73)	Director of Social Services, Swansea County Borough
DR I B SUTHERLAND	Senior Administrative Medical Officer, South Western Regional Hospital Board
MRS A WILLIAMS	Senior Social Worker, Morgannwg Hospital
MISS P H F YOUNG	Director, Central Council for Education and Training in Social Work

Departmental Members:

MRS E O JAMES	Welsh Office
MR R L JONES	Welsh Office
MR R A BIRCH	Department of Health and Social Security
MISS R M FURNIVAL	Department of Health and Social Security
MR J HALLOWELL (appointed 7.11.73)	Department of Health and Social Security
MR I JEWESBURY	Department of Health and Social Security
DR J T JONES	Department of Health and Social Security
MISS A M LAMB	Department of Health and Social Security

MRS D OTTLEY	Department of Health and Social Security
MR W D PAGET	Department of Health and Social Security
MR M W PERRY	Department of Health and Social Security
MR A F TAGGART (resigned 7.11.73)	Department of Health and Social Security
Secretary:	
MR P D WATSON	Department of Health and Social Security
Observer:	
MISS M M McINNES	Scottish Education Department

CONTENTS

INTRODUCTION

(i) The Secretary of State for Social Services announced in Parliament on 28 March 1973 the Government's decision that social work support for the health service in England and Wales should from 1 April 1974—the date of local government and NHS reorganisation—be provided by local authority social services departments. Hospital social workers should from that date be employed by local authorities and made available to the health service.

(ii) This announcement followed a period of controversy, during which the main issue of principle—whether the NHS should look to local authorities for social work support, or continue to provide a separate service of its own—was considered at length by the Working Party on Collaboration. A full account of that Working Party's conclusions has been published:* it reached a majority view that social work support for the NHS should be the responsibility of local authorities. The objective of NHS reorganisation was to provide an integrated service better adapted to meeting the health care needs of individual patients and of the community as a whole. Improved co-ordination of NHS and local authority services to provide a comprehensive system of care embracing health, social work and other community services was a central theme of this reorganisation, and the Working Party on Collaboration had been appointed to review the whole question of links between NHS and local authority services. They concluded that collaboration between the two services would develop most effectively if the professional skills on which they relied were concentrated in the most appropriate service—medical, nursing and dental skills in the NHS, and social work skills in the local authority. This would promote the best development of professional skills and the best deployment of scarce professional resources to meet the needs of patients. Each service should rely on the other for the skilled help it needed.

(iii) The decision finally taken was based on consideration not only of the Working Party's conclusions, but also of a considerable volume of subsequent representations and comment. It was clear that there would be much unease in both medical and social work circles about the decision; and in announcing it the Secretary of State, following a suggestion in the report of the Working Party on Collaboration, said:

> "We propose to set up a broadly-based working party, representing both health service and local authority interests, to examine the practical arrangements for the provision of social work support for the health service by the local authorities."

He added that the local authority associations had given assurances that local authorities would await the conclusions of the working party before taking any action in relation to the responsibilities they would assume for hospital social work.

*Working Party on Collaboration: Report on activities to the end of 1972—HMSO, price 85p.

(iv) This is the background to our work. Our membership was chosen not merely to include representatives of both services, but also to give some expression to the views of those in both the health and social work professions who were known to be uneasy about the change. We have concentrated as much as possible on practical issues, since this was our appointed task. The scope for more wide-ranging discussion has, in any case, been severely limited by constraints of time. We have had a tight timetable to work to, in order to complete our discussions by the time of reorganisation, and this has led us to try to avoid discussion at too abstract a level of theory about the nature of social work, teamwork in health care, inter-professional relationships, and so on. These are fruitful areas for debate and controversy, which could have occupied us for far longer than the time available to us. We have necessarily touched on them: but to no greater extent than seemed necessary for our purpose of offering guidance on practical issues arising from the reorganisation. In other words, we do not pretend to have written a textbook on social work and the health service.

(v) Within these limits, however, we have been able to consider a considerable volume of written evidence presented to us, and we have made a number of visits to look at experience in the field. We are grateful for all the help we have been given; and while our views on the more contentious aspects of this topic can hardly please everybody, we hope this report will show that we have paid careful attention to all the evidence presented to us.

(vi) Our experience during our work has led us to believe that some clearing of the air is needed if authorities and professional staff are to work in satisfactory partnership in this very important area where health and social care are inextricably linked. There are misunderstandings on both sides, and differences of view on both professional and organisational issues. We have thought it right to try to bring at least some of these out into the open, and to do so in a way that may help to put them into perspective and promote better understanding. We hope that as a result this report may provide a basis for constructive local discussion of the new systems and methods of working that will have to evolve.

(vii) Because of pressure of time and the need for early guidance to field authorities we have, in advance of this report, given advice on three topics:

(*a*) Arrangements for transfer of staff at the appointed day. We made this our first priority, since early guidance was needed on arrangements for determining to which local authorities hospital social workers should transfer. Our views on this were incorporated in a consultative document issued by the Department of Health and Social Security and the Welsh Office on 1 November 1973; and following that consultation the necessary staff transfer order has been made.*

* National Health Service (Transfer of Social Services Staff) Order 1974 Statutory Instrument No. 318—circulated with LASSL(74) 7 and DS 50/74 (Welsh Office Circular 81/74).

(b) Appointment of a senior officer in local authority social services departments. The Working Party on Collaboration had recommended that each local authority should arrange for a senior officer of their social services department to be specially responsible, under the Director of Social Services, for the provision of social work support to the area health authority. This recommendation had been approved by the Government, and commended to local authorities, before we began our work. We felt that guidance on this post, and on the type of person to fill it, was needed to assist local authorities in making this important appointment in advance of the appointed day. We therefore submitted a statement of our views at an early stage in our work, and in the light of this the Department of Health and Social Security and the Welsh Office issued guidance to field authorities on 31 December 1973.*

(c) Management and organisation of social work support for the health service. We were very conscious that field authorities and staff, as the date for reorganisation approached, were anxious to know as quickly as possible our conclusions on the way in which the services should be organised in the future. We therefore produced an interim report on this topic which the Department of Health and Social Security and the Welsh Office circulated on 5 March 1974.**

The topic at (a) was a once-for-all transitional matter, and we do not deal with it further in this report. But our views on (b) and (c) are now embodied in this report, and form the substance of Chapter 5.

(viii) A report of this nature should not need a glossary. But we have found a number of points over which terminology can cause difficulty and—if only to avoid tedious and repetitive qualifications throughout the report—we think it will be useful to include in this introductory section some explanation of a number of points of usage.

(ix) *Social work "support" for the health service.* The word "support" has been criticised as implying that social work has only a supporting role to play. This view—expressed to us with most force by a doctor, not a social worker—reflects a fear that the particular contribution of social work within a clinical team was being undervalued by the very title of the Working Party. We hope it will be clear from what follows that we do not use the word with any implication that it relegates social work to a secondary position. We are at pains to point out, on the contrary, how the two systems of health and social services should support (help, assist, reinforce) one another mutually. This is support between equal partners with distinct contributions to make to a common purpose.

(x) *The hospital and the community.* We recognise that it is wrong to set these two words in opposition in a way that suggests that a hospital is not part

* LASSL(73) 47; Welsh Office Circular 5/74.

** LASSL(74) 5; Welsh Office Circular 73/74.

of the community it serves. Nevertheless, central to our study is the proper relationship between staff and services based in hospital and those based outside. If we appear to err at places by drawing a false distinction between the hospital and the community, this is merely because some convenient shorthand formulation is needed. We have, particularly in Chapter 5, to deal with a practical problem of linking up teams in social services departments on the one hand with health care teams and specialist health services on the other. In this context we have to distinguish between the hospital and the "community" teams. No offence is meant.

(xi) *The "area team*". This term is well understood in local authority social services departments: it is an operational group of social workers concerned with a defined geographical area within the local authority. This is the standard form of organisation for local authority fieldwork services. We have detected some uncertainty in health service circles whether this bears any relation to the "Area Team of Officers" as they understand it. The answer is that it does not. The area team of officers is the group of top officers serving an area health authority, within the new management structure of the NHS. When we use the term area team, we are referring to the unit of organisation within the local authority social services department covering a defined territory.

(xii) *Health care teams*. Both in hospital and general practice care of patients is recognised as being a task for teams involving nurses and other professional staff as well as doctors. In this report we are using the terms "clinical team" for the team in hospital and "primary health care team" for the team in general practice. (These should not be confused with "Health Care Planning Teams", which are something different again. Within the new management structure of the NHS they are to be responsible at health district level for advising management on the organisation and development of health services for particular client groups in the community.) Much of our discussion has been about the position of social workers as members of these teams; and while we have inevitably concentrated on their relationship to doctors, we are quite as concerned with their links with nurses and other team members.

(xiii) Finally, we must make it clear that questions of pay and grading for hospital social workers transferring to local authority employment are outside our terms of reference. These are matters for negotiation within the established machinery for local government service—the National Joint Council for Local Authorities' Administrative, Professional, Technical and Clerical Services. We are aware that they are considering these matters and we must leave it to them to resolve the issues that arise—while expressing the hope that staff anxieties will soon be resolved by early decisions.

CHAPTER 1
THE REALITIES OF COLLABORATION

1. The broad aim of collaboration between health authorities and local authorities is not controversial. The reports of the Working Party on Collaboration* discuss many possibilities for the co-ordination of services and the sharing of skills and resources in ways which can be to the advantage of both sides. But habits of joint working and joint planning will not come easily or without deliberate effort. In our study we have been looking at collaboration at its basic level—the working together of people of different professions in service to patients and clients. The organisational arrangements that have been adopted to promote collaboration in management and planning—matching of area health authority and local authority areas, Joint Consultative Committees, and so on—are important, since without them the two separate systems will lack the necessary framework within which collaboration can develop. These arrangements can promote a climate for collaboration. But they will not succeed unless there also develops a habit of collaboration between doctors, nurses, social workers and others in day-to-day working. This rests ultimately on the growth of understanding and confidence between individuals.

2. All our experience during our work, both in visits and in discussions, has tended to throw into relief differences in attitudes and expectations which can only be obstacles to true collaboration at this basic level. Fortunately these are matched by much goodwill and a genuine anxiety to break down barriers and to see services interlock better. While much of our work has necessarily been concerned with questions of organisation and management, we have also been told a good deal about the "facts of life" at working level: we hope that some initial reflections on these will help towards the development of new habits of mind and better understanding.

3. Changes in professional attitudes will take time, and perhaps the first general point to be made is that the world will not have been changed on 1 April 1974. But changes will have to follow in the following months and years if the full benefits of collaboration are to be seen in better care of individual patients. Reorganisation is a catalyst which will precipitate many changes: part of our object is to expose some of the issues which we think members of the various professions should bear in mind as they adjust to the new situation.

* In addition to the Working Party's report on its activities to the end of 1972, referred to in paragraph (ii) of the Introduction, a second report covering the Working Party's further work up to July 1973 has been published. A third and final report will be published shortly. Topics covered in these reports include:

First report	—	machinery for collaboration sharing of professional skills environmental health services school health services
Second report	—	supplies services building and engineering services management services and statistics ancillary services
Third report	—	financial arrangements arrangements for collaboration in London

4. Reorganisation—as social services departments already know and the NHS will now be discovering—is a traumatic process. NHS reorganisation will undoubtedly impose strains on the health service in the period ahead, while the social services have to cope with a second round of changes following local government reorganisation. During this period of change there is increased scope for misunderstanding, and each side will need to appreciate the problems of the other as it adjusts to its own new situation. Further, each side starts with a quite different style of management, and a quite different legacy of tradition in policy making and practice.

The Seebohm reorganisation

5. The 1970 reorganisation of the local authority social services brought changes of a kind which those outside the services may not fully understand. This was not merely an administrative upheaval. It had fundamental implications in both structural and professional terms for the organisation and delivery of an ever-widening range of social services. It has been followed by some disenchantment among doctors and social workers about what they see as the consequences of Seebohm, and about shortage of resources; and many hold doubts about the capacity of the new social services departments to meet the needs of the NHS for social work support. The social services world is still working through the process of building a system markedly different from what had gone before and developing a new service. Demands on the social services have mounted rapidly, partly through public expectations aroused by the establishment of the new service and partly through increased obligations imposed by legislation. The new departments, at a time when they have had to cope with the stresses of successive measures of reorganisation, have also been expected to discharge a much wider range of responsibilities than their predecessors—towards the chronically sick and disabled, children in trouble, the elderly, the mentally ill and handicapped, and the homeless.

6. These new responsibilities are being tackled by a service which operates from a resource base very different from that of the NHS. Direct comparison between the two services is difficult. It is not a case of comparing like with like—there are inherent differences in the nature of the services. The NHS is a distinct service directly funded by the Exchequer: local authority social services are one element only in a complex pattern of local services funded by local rates and central government grant. For both services manpower is a key resource, and manpower shortage a crucial constraint in development: but the social services are at a much earlier stage than the NHS in developing their training and organisational arrangements to meet their manpower needs.

7. What is noteworthy, however, is the rate at which the personal social services have grown since their reorganisation following the report of the Seebohm Committee.* Local authorities have shown strong commitment to this new service. In the successive annual negotiations of central government grant to local government (the rate support grant) central and local government have together agreed to make provision for the growth of the personal social

* Report of the Committee on Local Authority and Allied Personal Social Services—July 1968 (Cmnd 3703).

services at a high rate—more than double that for local authority services as a whole over the past three years. The agreed figure has been of the order of 7%—10% during this period, and the Government has made its contribution on this basis. But actual expenditure by local authorities has in fact run well ahead of this—in the region of 15%—to the extent that it is at risk of outstripping resources of manpower. There are local variations in the quality of the service, but there is no lack of will among local authorities generally to develop this service, and to give it high priority.

8. We think it right to record this because we are aware that development of the new social services departments has been seen by many critics in the health service as leading to less effective co-operation between members of the health professions and social workers in the care of the sick and handicapped. On the other hand social services departments, in seeking to meet their responsibilities to health services, are not always aware of the image held of them by many in the health service, and it may be useful to set out some of the problems which have been brought to our notice.

9. In the field of mental health, doctors were accustomed to working with a small number of specialist officers. Now they may find that their contact has to be with a much larger number of staff in social services departments, many of whom have little or no skill or experience in mental health matters. Health service staff have also been disconcerted by the extraordinary degree of staff mobility which has prevailed through the period of reorganisation and does not yet appear to have come to an end. In the process of setting up new departments and establishing structures with an enlarged hierarchy of managerial posts, there has inevitably been much movement of staff between departments and authorities. Many doctors feel they can hardly expect to see the same social worker twice. With local government reorganisation still to be worked through, this period of unsettled staffing may well persist for some time after 1 April 1974.

10. Much of this mobility has been upwards. In manning the new departments many senior posts have had to be filled, and experienced or trained social workers have been at a premium. Promotion has been widespread and often rapid. As experienced staff have been appointed to higher posts they have withdrawn from fieldwork and operational contact with other professions. The "front line" has increasingly been manned by the new entrants to a rapidly expanding profession. In health service circles there is a widely held view that local authority social workers are predominantly young and inexperienced. This overlooks the fact that social services departments contain large numbers of mature and experienced staff, and will continue to recruit them. Nevertheless it is true that social work is a young profession which is growing fast, and that the basic grades have many young, newly-qualified or unqualified staff. These are the grades with whom doctors are most closely concerned, and they are understandably worried at a situation in which a high proportion of experienced staff in those grades appear to have been promoted into managerial and supervisory posts, so that they are no longer in touch with them in day-to-day working. Hospital and family doctors see a system which differs from that with which they are familiar, where professional practice up to the highest level of seniority usually involves continuing contact with patients. This withdrawal

of experienced staff from the front line also worries many social workers, who feel that their professional skill is not being used to the best advantage, and that if the standard of professional practice already developed in the health services is to be maintained and improved some means will have to be found to enable senior members of social services departments to participate in direct service to clients. These are issues of considerable importance which should be given further consideration as the manpower situation in the social services moves towards greater stability and balance between experienced staff and the inexperienced new entrant. Meanwhile there is need for greater understanding of current problems, and our present purpose is simply to record this as an area for mutual tolerance until circumstances permit a more rational approach to the allocation of work at various levels of experience, seniority and skill.

11. Discussion of the Seebohm reforms inevitably leads on to the issue which bedevils medical/social work relationships above all others at present—the nature of the so called "generic" or generalist social worker. It is widely believed to be of the essence of Seebohm that every social worker should profess a general competence in all aspects of social work practice and eschew specialisation. This leads to an apprehension that the future of the social services lies with "general practice" social workers who are jacks of all social work trades—with the inevitable corollary. For social work in a hospital setting the future is feared to be a watering down of specialism and a loss of skills which doctors have learned to recognise and value.

12. The specialist versus generalist issue is one of much current debate among social workers, and in the present transitional stage there are varying approaches to it in different social services departments. We understand it to be a key issue for the future and for the future shape of training: and as such it raises issues going far beyond our terms of reference. *But it appears to us that there is nothing in Seebohm to imply the wholesale abandonment of specialism in social work practice.* The aim of the Seebohm report was the establishment of a family service—one door to knock at—competent to deal with all the inter-related social problems of a person in his family setting. This does not postulate a service in which every trained social worker possesses that competence in full, or possesses it to the same degree. We would think that an unrealistic and impracticable aim. No doubt the new service requires a greater breadth of common knowledge across a wider range of social problems than social workers normally possessed before Seebohm. We understand that social work training is moving in that direction. But practice continues to recognise a need for specialisation, and the trend in the field at present is most strongly towards the generic team of workers who between them possess a sufficiently broad range of skills to be able to provide a full service to their community, reinforced by specialist consultants and resources as necessary. Even in those areas where there is the strongest commitment to generic working, it must be remembered that trained social workers will have spent as much as half their training working under supervision in particular social work settings—possibly in hospital or in general practice—and will thereby have acquired some specialised knowledge in their basic training, and perhaps an inclination towards one branch of social work rather than another.

13. Thus the apprehensions of many doctors about the type of social worker they will have to work with in future may be needlessly pessimistic. As in all professions, the competence and knowledge of individual officers will vary; and until the new service has had time to settle down many officers will be working in unfamiliar situations. If the result of the transfer of responsibility for hospital social work—as is intended—is to extend gradually the social service support offered to the health service and to introduce it where it is now absent, then it follows that many social workers will be undertaking work in this field for the first time and will need time to gain experience of it. Factors of this kind are more likely to account for any initial difficulties rather than considerations of social work theory or a reluctance on the part of social workers to acquire special understanding of the needs of the health service.

14. In later chapters of this report we return to the questions of specialism in health service support and the implications for training. It is sufficient to say here that our enquiries have led us to the conclusion that *the health service will continue to need the support of social workers with specialised skills in working alongside health service staff in health settings. There must be no question of these skills being dissipated or devalued in the future.* The planned developments in the training of social workers are not designed to produce generalists to a standard pattern. Social workers with special skills appropriate to work in health and other settings will continue to be trained and employed by local authority social services departments.

The personal touch

15. One "fact of life" has impressed itself on us with especial force. Difficulties between two systems and two professions can be reduced by suitable organisational arrangements, and by better understanding of background issues such as those we have just outlined. But in the end effective partnership in the care of patients rests on personal understanding and co-operation by individual doctors, nurses and social workers.

16. Mutual understanding and respect between individual practitioners develops easily and productively where there is week-by-week contact over a considerable period of time. Doctors learn to know when social work can contribute to patient care and what can reasonably be expected from it, and social workers learn to carry out their work in a manner appropriate to the particular medical situation. We have already noted the professional partnerships which were common in the mental health field, where teamwork has been a feature of in-patient care in hospital, and in general practice family doctors and mental welfare officers built up working relationships based on mutual confidence. There is an important implication here for the way in which services are organised. *Arrangements designed merely to establish that a social worker can be called in when necessary by impersonal communication from one system to the other are not good enough.* Casual and infrequent contact between a doctor and a number of different social workers is not likely to promote effective co-operation; indeed it may, as we have been told, lead to a failure to

attempt communication, with consequent lack of services to patients and families at the time when they are most needed.

17. An important objective of the collaboration arrangements is to develop better and more comprehensive social support for the health service in ways that have not been possible in the past. Some hospitals, and the vast majority of family doctor practices, have not had social workers based on the premises or allocated to work with them from social services departments, either because none were available or because the need has not been acknowledged. It follows that we should look for measures which will encourage the health service to seek support and use it properly, and the social services to give it the right amount of priority amongst the total demands on their resources. It is obvious that circumstances will generally not permit a system where one doctor will always be able to work with the same social worker, but *we think it is possible and desirable to devise arrangements for doctors to communicate with the social services through a personal link well known to them and readily accessible. Similarly there should be a known channel for communication between social services and primary health care teams* in health centres and practices, or clinical teams in hospital, for discussion of the total need for social support and the best means of organising it. Within this framework it will be possible to develop teams of individuals working together on a regular basis.

18. An important point in this connection is confidentiality. This is often made an issue of great consequence when problems of inter-professional working are discussed, and it can all too easily be represented as a practical restraint on collaboration. It is a professional issue with implications going well beyond our terms of reference, and we recognise that it is a matter for serious concern among the professions to find acceptable solutions which protect the right of the individual to confidential communication with any professional person with whom they are in contact. But we can record as a matter for encouragement the fact that at no point in our discussions has it been suggested to us that confidentiality presents any real difficulty in working relationships between doctors and social workers provided there is personal confidence between the professionals concerned. Reservations about sharing information obtained in professional confidence occur on both sides, and the information on a social worker's file can be quite as sensitive as that in medical and nursing records. *For the needs of the patient to be fully understood, however, it is clearly right that medical and social information about him should be shared as far as necessary between those who are sharing in the task of caring for him.* Our impression is that this is already happening wherever doctors, nurses and social workers have established habits of joint working on a personal basis, and that no inhibitions are felt about it.

19. This reinforces the case for developing personal relationships between individual practitioners—what we have referred to as the personal touch. Through such relationships it is possible for doctors, nurses and social workers to tackle problems of patient care as a team. We regard this as a major object of the whole exercise. The needs of patients will be best identified and served if there is a genuine inter-professional partnership with each member of the

team making his appropriate contribution to the pattern of care. Such teamwork is already a feature of the work of the health professions, and in many hospitals social workers are already full members of the clinical team. *The future development of social work support for the health service should build on this pattern of teamwork and seek to extend it to areas where it does not exist.*

CHAPTER 2
SOCIAL WORK AND THE CLINICAL TEAM

20. There are widely differing attitudes to the idea of teamwork between the health and social work professions. At one extreme are those doctors who, if not antipathetic to social work, at least remain sceptical of its value to their patients and do not go out of their way to ask for it. At the other are those social workers who are so anxious to avoid any impression of medical domination that they are reluctant to work in close partnership with doctors. There is also a contrast of extremes between doctors who perceive social work assistance solely in terms of arranging for aids, equipment or accommodation, and social workers who are only concerned to offer assistance in terms of "psychodynamics, often forbiddingly expressed" (to adopt a phrase from the Seebohm report). Before effective partnership between social workers and other professions can exist, there must be clarity about what social work has to offer.

21. In many cases the appropriate contribution by the social worker may be at a comparatively unskilled level: the patient may need to have accommodation arranged, or a home help, or meals on wheels, or some physical facility in his home. The social worker in this situation needs to know how to "work the system" of the social services department in order to arrange what is necessary. But this is not a task calling for a high degree of social work expertise, and it can often be perfectly well handled by untrained staff or assistants.

22. One of the main problems for social services departments at the present time is to decide how best to use the skills of trained and qualified social workers, who are still a scarce resource. Much thought is being given to the allocation of less skilled work to assistants and untrained staff, and it will be unreasonable for doctors to assume that the only help worth having is that of a fully qualified social worker. The medical and psychiatric social workers with whom hospital doctors have mainly worked in the past contained in general a high proportion of trained and professionally qualified staff. The community-based teams of many social services departments at the present time are likely, by contrast, to include numbers of professionally unqualified staff. But these often bring great experience to their task and are fully competent to pay a valuable part as members of clinical teams, facilitating access to the resources of their departments. (It has become evident to us that there is among health professions much uncertainty about the nature of the training and qualifications which social workers may possess and about the position of untrained staff. For this reason we have thought it helpful to include information about this in a later chapter on training).

23. Thus part of the social worker's role in a team will be to give access to the various services of the local authority, and to arrange for the provision of assistance through the resources of the social services department itself or some other social agency. This is a most important task, which is not beneath the professional dignity of the most skilled and highly trained social workers. But it is by no means the whole of the contribution that social workers can

make. Just as it will be wrong to assume that a high degree of professional qualification is needed to mobilise the facilities available in a social services department, so it will be wrong to assume that this is all that social work has to offer. Despite long experience of social work in hospital settings, there is still evidence of doctors looking for little more than assistance with "goods and services" from their social work colleagues. The social work profession is itself very sensitive on this issue, and much of the evidence submitted to us has betrayed great anxiety that the proper role of social work in a health service setting should be clearly identified and set out, so that it can be fully developed for the benefit of patients and families in the new situation.

24. We received a statement from the British Association of Social Workers about this, from which the following is a quotation:

> "Much has been written since the appointment of the first almoner in 1895 to demonstrate the close connection between a person's physical, social and emotional functioning, and the value to be derived from close and effective co-operation between the social work and health professions, particularly the medical profession. The social worker's contribution broadly lies in assessing and interpreting the patient's environment, his attitude towards it and towards his illness, and the relationship between them, as well as in planning and carrying out treatment, after-care and rehabilitation. Detailed and specialist knowledge of the patient's personal history, his family relationships, his employment, his functioning in society and his attitude to illness, are of considerable importance when making a medical diagnosis."

25. Observing that past experience has been very largely with patients in hospital, and that support for patients in general practice has, with a few notable exceptions, been virtually non-existent, the Association describes the task for the social worker in hospital as follows:

> "Many (patients) need help to tackle the social and emotional problems which complicate ill-health and its treatment, which can affect the sick person at any stage of his illness. They may contribute to the causation of disease or arise from it. Anxiety concerning personal problems may impel a patient to postpone or refuse treatment or may retard progress towards recovery. The illness or admission to hospital of one member impinges on the whole of his family. Social work support may be needed equally for the patient and for his family. It is the view of members of the Association that social workers with experience in the hospital service should extend their responsibilities as soon as possible to cover the whole of the reorganised health service, and that attention should be given particularly to developing a service in hospitals, whether general, psychiatric or mental handicap, where there is at present none. Social work should also be developed in general practice, where there are likely to be special opportunities for early preventive intervention."

Many of those who made their views known to us stressed the need for social workers in health service settings to have the requisite knowledge, through training and experience, of the psycho-social implications of ill-health or handicap, and the skill to interpret this for the benefit of the patient and his family and for the rest of the health care team. In some cases very specialised knowledge of the type of disease and its likely process and outcome may be essential for this purpose.

26. It is not easy to describe briefly what the social worker's role entails in day-to-day work in support of the health service, because a wide variety of situations have to be covered. First, the work varies considerably according to the health service setting. It may, for example, be carried out in a hospital giving treatment for acute illness; in one providing long-stay care for the severely handicapped; in a teaching hospital; in a health centre; or in a family doctor's practice. Second, the nature of treatment methods employed affects the nature of the social work task. For example, in a coronary care unit the task will vary according to whether policy of the physician tends towards early mobilisation or prolonged bedrest. Third, in some specialised units such as radiotherapy, renal dialysis, terminal care, addiction units, or secure units in the mental health field, highly specialised social work functions may be required to meet the needs of the particular patients. Very specific social work skills have been developed in psychiatric units for children and adolescents, where the emphasis is on developmental and behavioural problems in a family setting, and where specialised problems of a psychiatric nature in young people are under investigation. Finally, in all these settings social work functions change as new knowledge affects treatment methods and the organisation of medical care.

27. Inside hospitals many different calls may be made on social workers. They may be needed on the wards, in out-patient clinics, or in day hospitals and other extra-mural facilities. They may be called in at any point in the period from before admission to final discharge, according to the needs of the patient and his family, or according to the need of the clinical team for advice and assistance on social aspects of his care. In some hospitals only a proportion of the patients will need their help: in others the majority will do so at one time or another. Their work with patients may be spasmodic; or it may be concentrated at those periods when personal problems, family problems, or problems of adjustment to a new situation are overwhelming. The help required may be short-term, when intervention at the time of crisis may suffice to enable the family to manage by itself; or it may be long-term when permanent disability is involved, or when progress towards recovery is obstructed by personal problems, whether emotional or practical in origin.

28. The social worker has a contribution to make to the work of the clinical team at various stages in the care of a hospital patient:

(i) *Diagnosis.* Assessment of the social factors involved may be an essential contribution to diagnosis, and this is a task in which social workers are much involved.

(ii) *Treatment.* Decisions on the best method of treatment, where alternatives are available, sometimes depend as much on social as on medical considerations. Medical services aim to provide the best known or best available treatment for the patient's complaints so far as they are understood. This may be ineffective or reduced in benefit to the patient if it is delivered without consideration of his way of life and his potential for adaptation in social terms. The patient may need re-assurance to dispel unwarranted fears, or support in facing unpalatable reality and practical assistance to make plans for changed circumstances.

(iii) *Discharge.* Decisions about the timing and arrangements for discharge from in-patient care should be made in full knowledge of the social as well as the medical situation of the patient. This can be a stressful time for him, especially after a long period in hospital or if he has to face changes as the result of illness or handicap. The family may also need a good deal of support. The social worker's function is to provide the team with a social assessment of any problems surrounding the patient's return home or to alternative residential accommodation, and to take any necessary action.

(iv) *After-care.* In some cases help may be required long after discharge from the hospital ward or clinic. Attempted suicide, abortions, non-accidental injury to children or wives, alcohol or drug abuse—these are all examples of situations where medical attention may be short-term but where the crisis has revealed a need for extensive social rehabilitation and therapy. Humane and effective care of the severely mentally handicapped, the young chronic sick, and the elderly with deteriorating mental or physical conditions requires long-term planning of complementary health and social care. Social workers share in the task of providing long-term support for such patients with general practitioners, health visitors, and community nurses.

29. In addition to providing a direct service to patients and families in association with other members of the clinical team, and advising on the social aspects of treatment, the social worker also has a responsibility to contribute to the team's approach to the organisation of patient care. The modern trend is for hospitals to become outward-looking and to regard themselves as an integral part of a total service to the surrounding community. The social worker can assist in this process through knowledge of, and contact with, a wide range of community services, including the voluntary organisations, and through awareness of social conditions in the neighbourhood as they change and develop.

30. Social workers also have an important training function in hospitals. Students of health disciplines add to the training they receive on the social aspects of health care the experience gained by working alongside social workers and learning from them. Social work students have to be given experience of acute and chronic illness in a hospital setting, and to learn from experienced social workers the skills needed to handle problems related to illness or handicap in families and to deal with the day-to-day emergencies to which they give rise. This is as important for those students who will eventually work in community social services as it is for those who will choose health settings when they qualify. Many community based social workers are dealing with socially inadequate families where mental health problems are a contributing factor, and their understanding can be incomplete without some degree of first hand

experience of caring for patients with mental illness or handicap in acute or severe form.

31. Outside hospitals, general practices and health centres offer new opportunities for social work participation and we consider the development of social work support for these services to be so important that we have given it separate attention in Chapter 3 of this report. Family doctors and the nurses working with them deal with a high proportion of health problems which do not require specialist care but persist, and seem to have their origin in personal maladjustment or family disharmony. Social work intervention can sometimes be effective in relieving stressful social situations with resulting improvement in health, or in arresting the development of more serious illness. Social workers can also complement medical and nursing care of mentally or physically handicapped people living at home by helping the family in various practical ways, or simply by offering a supportive relationship. They can contribute to health centre activities such as centres of the elderly or family planning clinics.

Teamwork in patient care

32. We have discussed the contribution that social work can make to the care of patients in terms both of providing support from social services and of providing professional skill in diagnosis, treatment and after-care. In doing so we have referred frequently to teamwork, and it should be clear that we see social work support for the health service largely in terms of associating social workers with health service professions in health care teams. What does such teamwork imply for the members of the teams?

33. *We suggest that teamwork in a clinical situation means that all members of the team accept that each has a professional contribution to make in his own right; and that it is both the right and, equally, the responsibility of each member of the team to make that contribution if the patient needs it. Such a responsibility derives not from the prescription of the head of the team, but from the right of the patient to have the benefit of all the team's skills as he needs them.* We believe that if these principles of teamwork are accepted then doctors, nurses and social workers will find it much easier to work together as partners than has sometimes been the case. In particular, the social worker will not feel that his access to the patient is contingent upon the direction of any other professional in the team (e.g. the doctor or the ward sister), but derives from his responsibility to the patient to make available the skills that he needs; conversely the other members of the team will feel entitled to rely on the social worker to take responsibility personally, or by liaison with other social workers, for the social work component of the needs of all of the team's patients. The definition of each member's contribution is a matter of negotiation between all members of the team. It will usually derive from a collective discussion of a case and an agreed apportionment of responsibility for different aspects of its management. The responsibility of each member is then to the team as a whole for the performance of the contribution upon which the whole team has agreed.

34. This may be thought a somewhat idealised approach which makes no allowance for the relative weight of the skills and experience of different professions. Within any such team the weight of the contribution made by

any individual member will, of course, depend on his personal capacity, knowledge and experience. Nevertheless, it is inherent in the idea of partnership between professions that none can prescribe to others in matters which lie within those others' professional competence. However senior a doctor and however junior a social worker (and the balance will not always be this way round) the relationship requires an acceptance that ultimately each professional is the best judge of what it is right for him to do and of the way in which he does it. These matters, of course, are open to discussion within the team and often other members can make contributions in each other's fields. Indeed, in the realities of the world it is quite likely that a junior social worker will often be particularly open to guidance from more experienced people in other disciplines just as a junior doctor often leans upon the experience of a more experienced ward sister or social worker. But the ultimate professional responsibility must be accepted as lying where it belongs—with the professional concerned, and where necessary with the more experienced senior staff who stand behind him. The social worker will also be well placed to advise the team of the availability of the social services department's resources, and this will sometimes mean that he will need to persuade the team to moderate its expectations for social services resources when it is clear that it is unlikely in a particular case that they can be met in full. But his judgement in these matters will be accepted by the other members of the team only if they have confidence in his being an effective advocate within the social services department for the team's share of its available resources.

35. Clearly, the development of teamwork to this degree implies a good deal of modifying of preconceived attitudes all round. The process is one of mutual learning; and it is encouraging to read, in one study of teamwork in general practice,* how this process can quickly modify attitudes among all members of the team and extend their respect for each other's expertise and functions.

> "Individual members of the team widened their concepts of their professional skills and discovered new delineations of roles; they also became more comfortable about interchange of functions. They adopted more flexible and imaginative attitudes towards the areas of client needs which are characteristically vague in primary medical care. At the same time everyone became more sharply aware of their individual skills. At the end of the project the early conflicts over rigid boundaries and functions of, say, health visitors and social workers appeared in retrospect so inappropriate that the team looked back at themselves with surprised amusement."

36. While it may seem a distant prospect, with present numbers of social workers, that this degree of teamworking can be developed throughout the health service, it should be the aim to work towards it as resources permit; and among the evidence submitted to us we can record a desire for it on the part of doctors. The British Paediatric Association have expressed—

* "Social Work in General Practice" by E Matilda Goldberg and June E Neil—National Institute for Social Work Training, 1972.

"an ungrudging recognition of the essential contribution of the social workers, . . . a desire to make clear the welcoming nature of our approach to social workers as a body, and our determination to see the reorganisation of the health services as presenting an opportunity to achieve the fuller and more effective co-ordination between our respective disciplines."

37. *To attain the degree of mutual respect on which teamwork must depend some basic rules of practice can, we think, be postulated.* They amount to no more than the common courtesies of teamwork—some practical questions of good manners: but they are extremely important.

38. *First, there must be some continuing personal relationship between individuals*—the personal touch we referred to in Chapter 1. Long-term relationships are better than short-term. A loosely-knit team with constantly changing membership will not function as well as a more settled one, or may not work at all.

39. *Second, regular opportunity for face-to-face contact by members is essential.* A voice at the end of a telephone is not enough. The team must get together regularly and on defined occasions for discussion, and to establish a background against which continuing informal contact can develop.

40. *Third, team members should report back to the team on action they take.* In the social worker's case this implies a routine procedure for ensuring that the up-take of a case is acknowledged; that the result of any action is reported back; and that closure of a case is recorded. In the doctor's case it implies a routine procedure for ensuring that the social services are given wherever possible warning of impending discharge or of approaching need for services, or of any substantial change which may affect the patient's situation or that of his family.

41. *Fourth, it should be recognised that priorities will often be differently assessed by different members of the team.* Doctors often have to make immediate decisions without waiting for an opportunity to consult other team members. If they do so on assumption that some supporting course of action by the social worker in their team will immediately follow, but have not consulted the social worker about it, there is obvious room for difficulty and disagreement. The snags lurking here are best faced openly, and there must be give and take on both sides. Social workers placed in this position should recognise the pressures on doctors to take urgent decisions, and should do their best to respond in the way expected, understanding the urgency felt by their colleagues in the team. Equally, their colleagues should recognise that lack of resources on the local authority side may make it impossible for social workers to meet the demands made of them as quickly as had been hoped. Local authorities, for their part, should recognise that the procedures of consultation and reference back which they often require of social services staff—particularly where the allocation of expensive resources is concerned—can lead to delays in resolving a case which may destroy confidence between members of a clinical team.

42. *Finally, the social worker attached to a team should not necessarily be expected to carry all responsibility for the social work follow-up of every case.* The aim of continuity of care should not lead to a presumption that every case must be handled by the team's own social worker. In many situations this will not be the best or most appropriate use of his skill or time, and it could well lead to his becoming overloaded and so causing delay. His duty to his team members is that he should keep them informed when he proposes to pass a case on, keep track of it through contact with the other social worker concerned, and report back on the outcome in due course.

43. All these ground rules are concerned, in one way or another, with aspects of communication between individual doctors, nurses, health visitors and social workers. When we come on to considering questions of organisation and management in Chapter 5, it will be found that communication is no less important an issue in the relationship between the two systems, NHS and local government.

CHAPTER 3
SOCIAL WORK AND PRIMARY HEALTH CARE

44. In Chapter 2 we drew attention to the importance we attach to the development of social work support for the family doctor services. In this chapter we give our views on the need for further experiment in the organisation of collaborative working between members of primary health care teams and social workers and social services departments. We are, of course, fully aware that trained social workers are in short supply and that the pressures on Directors of Social Services to provide social workers for teams working in various health and other settings are such that at the present time any large-scale expansion in full-time attachment to individual and group practices is unlikely. Nevertheless *we make a strong plea that experimentation in the field of social work and primary health care should receive urgent consideration by the professions and by the health and local authorities.* In this we reiterate the recommendations in the Seebohm Report (now five years old) that social services departments should make a determined effort to collaborate with local general practitioners, and that a variety of experiments in team work should be started.

45. A five year action study was begun in 1965 in a group practice in Camden and was reported in "Social Work in General Practice," by E M Goldberg and J E Neill.* This report provided us with valuable information on the way in which the multi-disciplinary team in that practice worked, the characteristics of clients referred for social work help, and the way the social worker's method of working evolved during the course of the project. The authors concluded that it was not necessarily the case that full-time assignment of a social worker should be made to every group practice, and they made several suggestions for alternative methods of promoting collaboration, which we hope will be adopted more widely. Health centres where numbers of family doctors work with supporting nursing and other health personnel are obvious sites for full-time attachment where resources permit, and *we hope that all new health centres will be designed to include accommodation for the use of social workers.* In smaller group practices arrangements can be made for regular consultations between the practice staff and social workers from the social services area teams, at which referrals can be discussed; some of these can then be dealt with on the premises, and others taken away for more long-term attention using the appropriate community resources. One suggestion of Goldberg and Neill which we thought of particular interest was that full-time attachment for a limited period would be justified in order to build up habits of joint working and create channels of communication between the staff of the practice and the social services department which would survive after a time on a less formal basis. This method would permit scarce resources to be spread more widely, and their use tested in various situations.

46. We know that a number of social services departments have already established a system of social work support for some practices and health centres, and that discussions between Directors of Social Services and family

* See reference at foot of page 23.

doctors are continuing. We offer some guidance which we hope will encourage and assist in this important area of professional collaboration. Whatever the methods of providing social workers for practices which can be adopted now, or made an aim for the future, it is important that the need for team work in this setting, and its advantages, should be fully understood by doctors, social workers and administrators of social services departments.

47. At risk of stating the obvious, we should remind social services departments that, with very rare exceptions, every individual coming to them for help is registered with a general practitioner. The problems which people have do not divide neatly into those resulting from ill health and those with social origin, though one may predominate at one time or another. Both health and social care in the community is moving towards the same objective—that of a family-based approach taking into account not only the needs of the individual but his social setting. At the very least, these facts establish the case for a vastly improved communication system between social services departments and general practices; and *the family doctor has an interest in being informed whenever patients on his list are receiving help from a social services department.*

48. On the other hand, the family doctor and his team are frequently the first point of contact for those seeking help with their social problems, and the person to whom other agencies (for example the police) or other people like relatives and neighbours may turn when someone is seen to be in difficulty. The medical content of the circumstances in which the doctor is approached may be minimal at the time, but potentially serious; and further *reference by a family doctor to a social worker may not only be appropriate to the patient's immediate needs, but may prevent the development of more complex situations of stress and breakdown in health.* Some situations can be met simply by the dispatch of information or by a letter or telephone referral. But there are others in which the nature of the problem may not be clear, or where medical and social factors are inextricably interwoven and may call for an integrated programme involving personnel from the primary health care team and from the social services department working together on behalf of an individual or family.

49. It is clear from studies of experimental attachments to individual and group practices that once there is a social worker working with a primary health care team and known personally to its other members, the number of referrals from the doctors or nurses for social work help increases rapidly, and genuine team work develops once there is mutual understanding of the part that social work can play in this setting. We do not think there are clear demarcation lines which can be laid down to distinguish the roles of the various professional members of every team in every practice. General practitioners vary in their method of working. Some for example regard counselling on personal and family relationship problems as their responsibility. Others would prefer to hand this over to a health visitor or social worker, or they may feel that the pressures of a busy practice do not allow them to undertake this time-consuming work to the extent that is required. We do not want to suggest that social workers should be included in practice teams to take over any part of

the doctor's work, or to relieve him of demands on his time. But we do think that *there are opportunities here, as in the hospital clinical teams, for the practice of complementary kinds and levels of expertise by members of a primary health care team which will lead to a more comprehensive service to their clients.* Doctors with experience of working closely with social workers have said that, far from saving medical time, the availability of a social worker sometimes increases their own involvement as a joint medical/social assessment of need may reveal a more complex situation than appears on the surface. They nevertheless stress the positive contribution such teamwork can make to the preventive aspects of family health care. As in the hospital setting, if the concept of teamwork between doctors, nurses and social workers is accepted as a collection of different professional skills put together in equal partnership, the various roles and responsibilities of each member can be easily worked out to fit individual inclination and ability, and to adapt to any special features of a doctor's practice.

50. The range of functions which can be carried out by social workers attached to primary health care teams has been identified in studies of experimental attachments, and can be summarised as follows:

(i) Social assessment and evaluation as a contribution to diagnosis. This includes investigation of the social setting—for example, the functioning of the patient in social and family relationships. Both health visitors and social workers can help in this, when knowledge additional to that the doctor already has is needed to clarify or enlarge the picture, or when assessment of these factors from a different point of view may assist a comprehensive diagnosis.

(ii) Application of social work to assist the treatment process. Various methods of therapeutic work may be employed, with individuals, with families, and with groups of patients; and work may be done individually or together with other members of the team.

(iii) Mobilisation of services from the local resources of social services departments and voluntary organisations and liaison with other local authority or government departments, e.g. housing, education, social security, the courts and probation service.

(iv) Educational work with the team on the significance of social factors in health care, including teaching and supervision of students working in the practice.

(v) Consultancy and advice for other staff in the social services department. This may involve advice on the care and handling of individuals and families registered with the practice, or more general advice on identification of local need for social services as revealed in the practice or health centre.

51. Research has also demonstrated, by analysis of the characteristics of those patients referred to an attached social worker, that certain groups are particularly likely to have social problems. The elderly, single, divorced or separated have been found to predominate, and many more women than men were referred for the social worker's help. Goldberg and Neill found also that

the occupational distribution of those referred reflected that of the neighbourhood, and that there was no undue weighting towards the less privileged social classes. This adds weight to our belief that general practice is a strategic place for identification of social problems among people who may at present not be coming to the notice of social services departments. Many of these people require a social rather than a medical solution to their difficulties in the long term, if not immediately—for example, to relieve the stress of loneliness and isolation, bereavement, or reduction in physical capacity such as loss of hearing and sight in the elderly. The assistance of a social worker brought in from outside the practice by a letter or telephone referral, is often rejected by the patient. But such help may become acceptable if it is offered by a person clearly seen by the patient to be a colleague of the doctor and nurse in the team.

52. Some doctors have found that the greatest social work contribution to the work of their practice has been in the area of mental ill-health or psychological disturbance, symptoms of which are found in a high proportion of their patients. Many of these patients do not require, or are not willing to accept, specialist treatment in a hospital or clinic, but they can be a tremendous burden in general practices. Social workers with particular training and experience in this area of work are probably needed to help with such cases, and these will certainly not be available in large numbers. But where there are doctors and social workers interested in developing a joint approach to problems of mental illness and psychological disturbance, we urge that further experimentation should be made in attachments giving sufficient time and continuity to allow for it.

53. We are aware that the number of family doctors anxious or willing to accommodate social workers within their practices is not proportionately very high at present. We believe however that interest is growing and we are impressed by the enthusiasm of those who have had experimental attachments and have written of their findings. Where there have been failures, the reason may be that plans for joint working have not been sufficiently discussed and mutual appreciation of the scope for social work as well as its limitations has not been established from the beginning. Directors of Social Services, too, have to be convinced that amidst all the other pressures on them, any priority they give to assigning staff to this work is justified by the results, and they may think that scarce social work resources should be deployed more, for example, in forging close links with schools rather than with general practice. Nevertheless, in the context of our study of social work support for the health service, we are in no doubt of the importance of developing this link between social services departments and general practice as rapidly as resources permit. In a field of discussion which has tended to be dominated by the question of hospital-based social work we wish to emphasise that *we see development of support for general practice as a priority for the future, since it presents a major opportunity for significant improvement in methods of health and social care.* We have deliberately chosen to present our views on this first, before going on to consider the position of the hospitals.

54. We hope therefore that discussion between doctors, nurses, health visitors and social workers, and between social services departments and area

SW—A4*

health authorities, will develop, and that opportunities will be taken to try out various methods of working together in the general practice setting. Perhaps the most important change needed is one that would influence attitudes. We believe that there are many misconceptions which would be reduced by more face-to-face contact anywhere where the professions meet together to discuss common objectives. Multi-disciplinary meetings and seminars are becoming more common in many areas of health and social services collaboration, and we hope that there will be an increase in those concentrating on the primary health care services.

CHAPTER 4
SOCIAL WORK IN HOSPITALS: SOME PRACTICAL EXPERIENCE

55. Even before 1 April 1974 some local authority social services departments were providing social work in hospitals. In some cases this was because the hospitals had not been able to make adequate arrangements themselves and had turned to the local authorities for assistance. In others there had been local agreement to explore the advantages of a more integrated social work system. We made a number of visits to discuss these arrangements locally, and found that they helped to clarify issues which local authorities and area health authorities will now need to face. In this chapter we discuss some of these arrangements, but it is not our intention in doing so that any one of them should necessarily be a model for action in other areas. Each context is in some way unique, deriving from local circumstances and preferences.

56. Some of the more general conclusions which we have drawn from these visits have already been set out in Chapter 1. But we have also been able to gain impressions of the practical problems of organisation and management that have arisen through different approaches. We have found there is no single solution; if we record that none of the schemes that we have seen appears to have solved all the problems, this is not intended as criticism. This is difficult territory, and it would be surprising if the first ventures into it had produced impeccable solutions. We have tried to derive from our visits some principles for the organisation of social work in health service contexts, and these are set out in the next chapter. But we have had to recognise limitations on the detail into which we could go; situations on the ground vary widely, in terms of organisation, resources and—it must be said—attitudes.

57. Differences in catchment areas will be a problem everywhere. Local authorities generally provide social services through teams covering defined geographical areas, while health care is normally provided by teams of doctors and nurses whose patients come from catchment areas which are less precisely defined. We found that where local authorities were already providing social work support for hospitals the problem of building links between health care teams in the hospital and the area-based social services teams outside had become a central pre-occupation, and we saw a number of different solutions, which are outlined below. Should the service be based on social workers in hospital or on area teams outside? And should the social workers dealing with cases in the hospital relate primarily to the area team structure outside, and so concentrate on cases coming from a particular area; or to the clinical teams inside, and so concentrate on cases dealt with by their teams regardless of where the patient comes from? When posed in sharp terms like these, with an implication that one or other course must be the right one, these questions are very hard to resolve satisfactorily, and we saw evidence of a number of difficulties ensuing when systems are evolved to provide a single answer.

58. These problems are less prominent in mental illness hospitals which operate in "divisions", each serving a defined part of the hospital's catchment

area. This arrangement has been recommended to hospital authorities as the first step in a long-term strategy of replacing large mental illness hospitals by local facilities in each district general hospital; and the hospital divisions are intended to look forward to this eventual arrangement by establishing links with the smaller catchment areas of future district general hospital units. Such steps offer the possibility of establishing some correspondence of catchment areas between the mental hospital divisions and social services areas, and one scheme on these lines is described below (Scheme E). But more commonly it has been necessary to explore support systems which have to cope with this problem of differing catchment areas. Our enquiries have shown that there are a number of possible approaches. We describe in the following paragraphs some of the possible solutions which we have seen.

Scheme A: Support from area team staff based outside hospital

59. It is possible to attempt to provide all support to the hospital from staff in area teams outside the hospital, who can come into hospital to deal with cases referred by clinical teams involving patients from their territories. We were told of one such scheme which had been abandoned because of complex problems of communication. The network was difficult to operate, and referrals had been made only for the more obvious practical services for which doctors saw a need. Social workers had had no opportunity to form personal links with health care teams or to become partners in these teams.

60. A modified version of this approach, while continuing to rely on staff in local authority area teams, tried to overcome the communication difficulty by assigning particular workers in the teams to particular groups of consultants. Under this arrangement the assigned social workers' time was divided; they were required to give about 70% of it to cases referred from their consultants, and 30% to cases referred from their area teams outside the hospital. As members of the area teams they were accountable to their team leaders and so, ultimately, to the Assistant Director of Fieldwork in the social services department. Outside that operational hierarchy there was a senior officer with an advisory role within the department's headquarters structure, experienced in hospital social work and responsible for co-ordinating the arrangements between the teams and the hospitals, and for providing professional consultancy. This system was designed to provide a personal contact for every health care team in the hospital and to devote a fixed share of the resources of each area team to support of patients in the hospital. The assigned social workers dealt with all referrals from their consultants, unless the patient was previously known to another social worker, in which case they passed it on. They also dealt with the longer term follow-up of discharged patients within their own areas, and passed on patients resident in other areas to colleagues in other area teams as appropriate.

Scheme B: Support from area team staff based in hospital

61. Another possible approach is to rely on support from area teams outside the hospital, but to have some detached members of those teams based in the hospital. We studied a scheme of this kind which had been negotiated between the hospital authorities and two local authorities in the hospital's

catchment area. There was an existing hospital social work department, and the agreed arrangements resulted in some—but not all—of its staff transferring to local authority employment and becoming members of the authority's area teams. These social workers remained based in hospital, and accepted all referrals from within the hospital of patients who came from their team areas. Thus their direct relationship was not with individual doctors but with the local authority area covered by their community-based teams; and they dealt with all hospital patients from that area, regardless of which clinical team was concerned. They could arrange for another member of their area team to follow a patient into hospital, if he was already dealing with him; and they could follow patients referred to them in hospital back into the community, calling on the resources of the social services department as full members of the area team.

62. Some features of this scheme should be noted. First, it had been introduced as the result of careful discussion between all the parties concerned, so that there was good understanding of its aims and methods and correspondingly less room for unreal expectations likely to lead to disappointment. Second, the scheme did not rely exclusively on social workers based in area teams. Those members of the hospital social work department connected with the geriatric and psychiatric departments remained as before working with particular clinical teams within the hospital. The system was mixed: all social work staff were based in hospital, but some medical specialties retained social workers working in direct association with the clinical teams, while others relied on workers linked with the local authorities' area teams. Third, there was a principal social worker available in the hospital to co-ordinate all social work activities as a focal point of contact for medical and nursing staff. She remained directly responsible for those staff working with doctors in the geriatric and psychiatric departments. Those linked with the area teams were not supervised by her, but by their team leaders. Nevertheless she was able to give them advice when necessary, and to give guidance to the local authorities' team leaders about their new responsibilities towards the hospital.

Scheme C: Support from separate hospital-based teams

63. An alternative pattern of support is that which relies on hospital-based teams of social workers to take all referrals within the hospital, their links being with hospital departments rather than area teams outside. In the example of such a scheme which we studied there were two such teams in the hospital. The local authority's services were organised on an area basis, each under an area director, and within each area there were a number of teams under team leaders. The two hospital teams were to be equal in status to these teams, and to be responsible for management purposes to one of the area directors. The hospital teams were to be linked with consultants and take patients referred by them without regard to the geographical basis of the area teams outside the hospital. Each hospital team would be dealing with patients from all parts of the local authority's territory, and working in parallel with all the area teams. Where a patient was already known to a social worker in an area team, he could follow the case into hospital. The staff of the two hospital teams could also follow their patients back into the community as necessary.

64. This scheme provides for a situation of complete overlap between the hospital teams and the area teams. The management of the interlocking pattern of communications that could result seems likely to call for a good deal of attention within the management of the social services department, and the intention was to appoint a principal social worker with special responsibility for health service support. This officer would not be responsible for managing the two hospital teams, since that task fell to one of the area directors, but would act as professional consultant to the hospital teams and as adviser on health service support generally to the local authority .

Scheme D: Support from hospital-based teams linked with area teams

65. We saw one scheme where the local authority and the hospital management committee had worked together to produce a service which integrated a hospital-based team with the area teams of the local authority social services department. The members of the hospital-based team were attached to clinical teams in the hospital; but each was also attached to an area team in the local authority fieldwork service. The social workers thus had affiliations both to clinical teams in the hospital and area social work teams outside. This dual responsibility was matched in the managerial structure of the social services department, where there was an Assistant Director (Medical Social Work) and an Assistant Director (Fieldwork). Under this system casework was categorised according to its main content as either hospital-based or community-based. For hospital-based casework the social workers' accountability ran through the senior member of the hospital social work team to the Assistant Director (Medical Social Work); for community-based casework it ran through the area team leader to the Assistant Director (Fieldwork). Within this system a hospital based social worker took referrals from the clinical teams to which he was attached; and if a patient lived in the area of his team outside, he kept the case for any further work needed after discharge from hospital. If the patient came from a different area, he passed the case to his colleague in the hospital team linked to that area. If the patient was already on the caseload of a social worker in an area team, that social worker could follow the case into hospital, and the hospital team could help to facilitate this.

Scheme E: Support for a large psychiatric hospital operating in "divisions"

66. This is the situation referred to in paragraph 58 above, where the problem of relationships between different catchment areas does not arise. In the example we studied, the catchment area of the hospital covered 6 local authority social services areas, and the hospital divisions were matched to those areas. One social worker from each area was made responsible for the social work of the clinical teams covering that area. The objective was to provide two social workers for each clinical team in the hospital, but this was far from being achieved. It had taken the local authority time to build up support to the extent of one social worker for each area, so that some teams were still having to share social workers. The social workers concerned were specialists, with experience and qualifications in the mental health field, who concentrated in the social work aspects of the psychiatric medical practices to which they were attached. They worked with the patients of those practices both inside

and outside the hospital, and thus had joint responsibilities to the health care teams and to the local authority area teams. They were not based in the hospital (with exception of one who had previously been based there and had continued working there), and much of their work was done away from the hospital. They attempted to share in the responsibilities of their local authority area teams by taking their turns at duty days and so on. As members of those teams they were within the management chain of command of the fieldwork services of the local authority. But the service they offered to the hospital was co-ordinated by a principal social worker at the headquarters of the social services department, who also offered professional consultancy and support to the social workers. He was not in the chain of management command for the area teams, nor a member of any of them; nor was he based in the hospital.

Discussion

67. We confined our visits to places where new models were being devised, to see what lessons could be learned. This led us to concentrate on the problem of linking hospital and community services, since this is the area of most evident difficulty. In the longer term we think that the reorganisation is quite as important in the scope it offers for linking social work with general practice. But there are unfortunately not many actual instances available for study at present.

68. So far as the hospital/community link is concerned, the systems we have seen have all tried different approaches to a similar objective. None has dismantled an existing hospital-based team, but each has explored a different way of establishing this link. They have demonstrated possibilities of basing staff either in hospital or outside, and of linking them either with clinical teams or area teams. It is early days to be sure that their pros and cons have been fully identified, but we have set out our impressions of them and we were helped towards our general conclusions by what we saw.

69. Of the five schemes reviewed above, Scheme C had made the least change from previous systems. Much planning had gone into this scheme, but we felt that there was still uncertainty about personal relationships which might present difficulty. There was intended to be a linkage between hospital and area-based teams, which were clearly seen as part of a single, integrated local authority service. But this rested on the fact that the two hospital team leaders were responsible to one of the area directors. Yet for most operational purposes it seemed likely that they would look to the principal social worker for health services for support and guidance. Their relationship with other area directors was unclear, and there was a risk that health service social work and community social work would develop on parallel lines with too little provision for linkage between them.

70. By comparison, Scheme D presented greater opportunities for integration, for it retained a hospital-based team, each member of which was attached both to a clinical team in the hospital and to an area team outside. But the dual accountability of the social workers could obviously create a good deal of tension if it were not managed with understanding on both sides, and it appeared to

rest heavily on the good-will of managers in the two parallel chains of responsibility. Much also depended on clarity about the split into hospital-based and community-based cases, and this was obviously difficult to regulate with any precision. The system appeared to be working well, through good co-operation on all sides, and to be giving satisfaction to the hospital staff, but we gained the impression that it had not achieved a very close integration of the services inside and outside the hospital. Possibly because of the potential complexity of the situation in which the hospital-based social workers were placed, it appeared that the traditional pattern of hospital-based social work had in practice not been significantly altered, and that the link with the area teams remained tenuous by comparison with the relationship with health teams in hospital. The system was explicitly designed to link the two together. It was still fairly new, and over a period of time it might well succeed better in this.

71. This scheme, as others we saw, gained much from the close personal attention from the Assistant Director (Medical Social Work), who had been appointed to set it up in the first place, and who was concerned to build up the necessary relationships for it to operate effectively. We found it significant that both she and her Director of Social Services thought that the creation of her post at a sufficiently senior level had enabled her to play a useful part in general policy discussion within the social services department, so that expertise in both hospital and community social work was brought to bear on the planning of services in areas where there were interlocking problems of health and social care. Integration of services at this level of management and policy formation is clearly as important as at the operational level.

72. Schemes A and E differed from Schemes C and D in attempting to organise social work for the hospitals in question wholly or mainly from area teams outside the hospital. A particular feature of Scheme A was the deliberate attempt to integrate those concerned with hospital cases fully into the area teams by giving them a share of other casework. This was welcomed by the social workers concerned, who appreciated the opportunity to operate within a social services department team. But the scheme was much criticised by consultants on the ground that their access to social work help was still not direct enough. Without any point of immediate contact with a social worker readily accessible within the hospital, they felt that the system remained anonymous and that communication was difficult. The social workers themselves felt some conflict in the demands made by their hospital and area responsibilities: some clients outside hospital presented immediately pressing problems which could hardly be ignored and might appear more acute than those of a patient in hospital. The consultants felt that in this situation of divided loyalties the hospital always came off second best. They had not had a strong social work department in the hospital previously, but there had at least been a social worker whom they could always contact and through whom liaison with the local authority services could be established. The situation appeared to be one where the local authority's efforts to provide a higher degree of support than the hospital had previously enjoyed were nevertheless encountering difficulties of communication. Until these were overcome, there would be insufficient confidence for effective team-working to develop.

73. In scheme E the social workers were not based in the hospital (with one exception), and did much of their work away from the hospital, sharing to an extent in the responsibilities of their area teams. They saw considerable advantage in this link with the teams, which kept them in touch with developments in social service provision and gave them access to the total resources of the local authority social services department. The link made it easy for them to hand on cases to other members of the teams if their caseloads became excessive, and to arrange for other team members to follow cases into hospital if they were already dealing with them. There were, however, problems for the social workers about sharing their time between the hospital and the community, particularly as they had to do a lot of travelling over long distances. For the doctors (who were generally appreciative of the scheme) it seemed that the social workers were not accessible enough: they would have preferred them to spend more time in the hospital, particularly at out-patient clinics. Consultants were anxious to work more closely with social workers: but the system was insufficiently developed—and did not provide enough manpower—for the social workers to be able to meet all the consultants' expectations. We saw this as evidence of a problem we met in a number of settings—a degree of disappointment with a new system because there had been high hopes of what a small number of social workers might be able to achieve. The risk in this situation is that the social worker, because he is neither regularly accessible nor able to provide all the services that the consultants would wish, fails to establish himself as a full member of the hospital team.

74. A difficulty in Scheme E, both for the co-ordinating principal social worker and for the social workers themselves, was that they appeared to be in a rather specialised position, not fully in the main stream of either a hospital-based or a community-based service, which made their career prospects within the structure of the social services department appear rather uncertain. On the other hand, this was a pioneering venture and we did not read too much significance into this. The most encouraging features of the scheme were the evident enthusiasm of the staff concerned for the opportunity it gave them to provide some continuity of service for the mentally ill both inside and outside hospital; and the wish of the consultants concerned to make full use of the service and to see it developed still further.

75. Scheme B, under which social work was provided by area team staff based in a hospital, seemed to us to be of particular interest. We found that the workers concerned were enthusiastic about the new arrangement, and the opportunity it offered to widen the basis of the support they could offer to other hospital staff, and to develop a more continuous pattern of care for their clients. Some consultants were less enthusiastic about the introduction of new arrangements which had broken the traditional pattern of attachment of social workers to clinical teams: they now had to deal with a larger number of social workers, according to the patient's home area. But there was much support from doctors for the new system. The period of careful preparatory discussion seemed to have helped in this, and also the retention by some medical specialties of social workers working directly with the clinical teams. The presence within the hospital of a co-ordinating principal social worker had also helped to gain

the confidence of doctors and her role appeared important as a facilitator of the new arrangements. Generally, although this was a new scheme, and it was too early to assess its effectiveness in all respects, it appeared to contain many good features; it was well prepared and flexible in operation.

76. Our visits showed us that the number of permutations possible must be very extensive. Future arrangements must take account of whatever system is already established locally. However, the long-term purpose of the reorganisation is that new models should be able to evolve and that no part of the social work services should be isolated from the rest. The schemes we have seen are all steps in a necessary direction; and they have helped us to form some broad conclusions, which are described in the next chapter.

CHAPTER 5
MANAGEMENT AND ORGANISATION

77. In Chapter 4 we gave an account of some existing experience in the organisation by local authorities of social work support for the health service. This had led us to formulate a number of general points of principle, on which we think any arrangements for managing and organising social work support for the health service must be based.

78. In the first place, *the over-riding objective should be to devise organisational arrangements which promote the integration of social work in support of general practice and hospitals with the full range of services provided by the local authority social services department. The aim should be continuity of care wherever the needs of the individual or the family indicate this: and the organisational structure should aim at integrating social work support for patients receiving health care within the fieldwork services of the department, rather than preserving them in a separate compartment.* Local circumstances, including the availability of resources and the nature of existing arrangements, are likely to indicate a number of local variations in the organisational pattern to be adopted. But we are of the firm view that these should be variants based on this general proposition rather than contrasting styles of organisation that take no account of it.

79. *A second main objective should be to promote teamwork between doctors, nurses and social workers.* We have already dealt with the question of teamwork in Chapters 2 and 3 and there is no need to repeat our views here at any length. Inter-professional partnership depends on confidence between individuals which cannot develop through impersonal arrangements providing merely for structural links between two organisations. Personal understanding between individual doctors, nurses and social workers must be the keynote, so that they can work together as a team.

Support for general practice

80. We have already emphasised in Chapter 3 the importance of the social worker's contribution to family doctors' practices, and to health centres. *In order to integrate such supporting social workers into the main structure of the local authority department, we are clear that any social workers attached to practices should be members of local authority area teams,* according to the location of the practices. But since general practitioners' patients do not come from defined catchment areas, *the arrangements should be flexible enough to allow attached social workers to care for patients coming from outside their own social services areas in appropriate cases.* It will be destructive of the team-working relationships between doctor and social workers if the social worker attached to a practice has invariably to pass on cases which come from the territories of other area teams. We understand that such flexibility of working across boundaries is not uncommon in local authority social services departments, and we urge its adoption in this case.

Support for hospitals

81. We have given considerable thought to the relative merits of basing social workers in hospitals or in area teams. The advantages of basing social workers in hospital must be set against the benefits which community-based social workers can bring in terms of continuity of care and breaking down the isolation of some hospitals from the community. A balance has to be struck, and we think that the determining factor should be the needs of particular patients, and of their families, and how these may best be met.

82. *The needs of patients in particular types of hospital provision justify the basing of social workers in hospital.* We have in mind:

(i) those specialties where the social component in treatment looms large (e.g. geriatrics, child health and psychiatry—including mental handicap) and calls for teamwork by social workers, doctors and nurses in diagnosis and treatment, which is best promoted by basing social workers in the hospital;

(ii) long-term treatment units (regardless of the nature of the medical specialty) which generate a considerable volume of social work within the hospital setting requiring the presence of social workers based in the hospital;

(iii) those highly specialised medical units which call for a specialised knowledge of the form of treatment, and for an immediate social work presence which can best be provided by someone based in the hospital.

We recommend that in these cases social workers should be based in hospital.

83. *Social workers may also need to be based in hospital for other purposes:*

(i) some social problems present themselves urgently in hospital and crises arising from illness need to be dealt with by a social worker immediately available.

(ii) some suitably qualified social workers need to be located in hospitals as a training resource, both for social work students needing practical placements and supervision in hospital settings and for medical, nursing and other health service staff needing some element of social work education as part of their professional training.

(iii) the medical, nursing and other staff in hospital need an accessible social work contact for purposes of general guidance on the social aspects of illness and handicap and on the availability of social services.

(iv) where a number of social workers are working with patients in hospital there is a clear need for someone based in the hospital to co-ordinate their activities, provide them with counsel and support, and act as a point for contact with hospital staff.*

84. We have not felt it right—or indeed feasible—to attempt to prescribe a comprehensive set of criteria for deciding where social workers should be

* It should be noted that the role described in this sub-paragraph relates to co-ordination of services within a single hospital. We identify later a separate co-ordinating role for a health district as a whole—see paragraphs 95-97. These two roles are distinct, though there may be circumstances in which it will be convenient to combine them in one person.

based: circumstances vary. But the examples in paragraphs 82 and 83 indicate the type of situation in which the patients' needs will be better met by basing some social work staff in hospital. For other patients, where the main need is to preserve continuity of social work care, and possibly to attend as much to the needs of other members of the family, support from workers based in area teams outside the hospital will be better. But in that case a great deal depends on establishing effective communications and working relationships between the social workers based outside the hospital and the medical, nursing and other staff inside. (We return to this question of communication below).

85. Thus *we think that a comprehensive pattern of social work support for hospitals should develop—as staff resources permit—on the lines of providing both hospital and community-based social workers in support of hospital teams,* the former concentrating their attention on situations where the main focus of social care falls within the hospital (as in paragraph 82) and on the type of tasks indicated in paragraph 83. But *whether social workers are based inside or outside hospital, working arrangements must permit those based in hospital to follow cases into the community, and those based outside to follow cases into hospital, wherever this is appropriate and best serves the patient's needs.* Whatever pattern of organisation is adopted, there should be conscious effort to achieve the flexibility necessary for this.

Linking the hospital and community care teams

86. *Joint Consultative Committees should particularly concern themselves with the problem of linking the hospital and community care teams, to ensure that arrangements appropriate to local circumstances are devised. They have been asked to set up special sub-committees to deal with social work support for health services, and these should make a point of ensuring that officers of the two services work out suitable local arrangements.* (There should be officers in both services with special responsibilities in this matter—see paras 92 and 93 below).

87. As described in Chapter 4, we have studied a number of solutions to this problem, and have found no single or simple solution. It has to be accepted that a neat pattern of correspondence between health teams within the hospital and social services area teams outside will not normally be feasible, except where a psychiatric hospital has been "divisionalised" and clinical teams are taking patients from defined geographical areas. From the solutions we have seen adopted in practice it is clear that problems arise if an attempt is made to rely exclusively on social workers from area teams based outside the hospital and dealing with hospital patients from their areas, regardless of which clinical team is concerned, since this means that doctors in hospital have to deal with a considerable number of social workers and are unable to develop a close working relationship with any. Conversely, a system which tries to rely exclusively on linking social workers with clinical teams will create difficulties in relationships between those social workers and others in area teams outside.

88. In general terms we suggest that the solution should:

(*a*) not lie in setting up a "separate hierarchy" of social work support for the health service outside the main structure of the fieldwork side of the social services department, since this will work against the integration of services;

(*b*) allow for a comprehensive support system embracing both hospital-based and community-based workers; and

(*c*) be capable both of providing individual health staff with constant points of reference and access to social services, and of facilitating entry of community-based social workers to care for hospital patients in appropriate cases.

89. *We therefore regard good communication between health and social services as the single most important feature for bringing the two services into partnership:* this is dealt with at greater length in the following paragraphs.

Communication

90. Under this heading we are concerned first with communication between the two systems—health and social services. There is a need for a clear pattern of communications at three different levels:

(i) between the local authority social services department as a whole and the area health authority (AHA);*

(ii) between the local organisation of the social services department and the health service at health district level; and

(iii) between individual social workers working in support of health services and health service staff.

Effective communication at each of these levels is needed to ensure that under the new system the best possible arrangements are made to preserve and carry forward the existing standards of service to which the health service is accustomed; and to lay foundations for the development of a closer involvement of the resources of the two services in mutual support.

91. There is also a question of communication within the organisation of the social services department, and in considering this, we find it necessary to distinguish two separate functions:

(*a*) that of *managerial* responsibility for organising effective social work support for health services; and

(*b*) that of *operational* accountability for the work done by individual members of a social services department.

The second of these functions (operational accountability) runs through the organisation from top to bottom, and occurs at all three levels described in paragraph 90. The first function (managerial responsibility) does not occur at level (iii), but is of particular importance at levels (i) and (ii). Given the diversity of organisational structures in local authorities, it is not possible to lay down a standard pattern for the deployment of staff to carry out these two functions. (At levels (i) and (ii), for example, they could be combined in a single person, or allocated to different people, according to what best fits the local organisation.) But there are some general principles to be established about the functions at

* In London this will sometimes be a question of communication between a single AHA and a number of social services departments. See also paragraph 98(*b*).

all three levels. We deal with each level separately in the following paragraphs, concentrating on the managerial function at levels (i) and (ii), and the operational function at level (iii). We then suggest what the implications are for the structure of social services departments.

Communication at top management level

92. It is a feature of the new management arrangements for the NHS that each AHA is appointing a specialist in community medicine and a nurse who will have special responsibility for arranging health service support for the local authority. These two officers will be concerned with planning health services for the elderly, the mentally ill and handicapped, and the physically handicapped. They will also advise the local authority on the health aspects of its responsibilities under the Local Authority Social Services Act, and ensure that the local authority obtains the health services support and advice it needs. They will have an important role in relation to the working of the Joint Consultative Committee; and they will need a clear point of contact at a senior level in the local authority social services department.

93. To match this, the Working Party on Collaboration, when proposing the transfer of responsibility for social work support for the health service to local authorities, recommended that in each local authority social services department there should be a senior officer with a special responsibility to the Director for arranging social work support for the area health authority and to be a point of contact for the AHA management in these matters.* This recommendation was commended to local authorities by the Department of Health and Social Security and the Welsh Office. In the light of our discussions about the nature of the task of the social work contribution to health care and our review of existing patterns of organisation and experiment in this field, we have considered what further advice needs to be given on this subject.

94. We think that the officer holding this appointment should be part of the senior management team of the social services department. It is not appropriate for him normally to be concerned with individual casework issues, or with professional consultancy and advice for social workers engaged in such work. His function is essentially that of managerial responsibility, as described in paragraph 91. *We recommend that the senior officer should be appointed near the top of the social services department to be responsible for arranging social work support for the health service, for discussion with the area health authority, and for the forward planning of services relating to the health service.*

He should be concerned with the whole range of social work and social service support for the health service. Because local authorities arrange their management structure in different ways, it would be inappropriate for us to propose a standard grading for this officer; but he should have sufficient authority and capacity to be able to give effective support to the health service, and to represent his department authoritatively in discussions with senior officers of the area health authority and the AHA itself, whether through the machinery for collaboration or otherwise. *Wherever possible, he should be professionally*

* See paragraph 5.26 of the Working Party's first report.

qualified in social work with an understanding of casework requirements, and should have some experience of the provision of social work in a health services context and knowledge of the particular problems and needs of the health service.

Communication at district level

95. We think there is also a function of managerial responsibility in respect of social work support for the health service to be carried out in health districts. As our enquiries have shown, many patterns of organisation of social work are possible in health districts; but common to all of them, in our view, is *the need for a professionally skilled officer of appropriate seniority to act as a central point of reference in each health district for the management of social work activity in support of the health district.* He should be responsible for ensuring the efficiency of the necessary links between the resources of the local authority social services department and the health service, and should also be able to act as a point of reference for the District Management Team of the health service on social service problems. We envisage that, as resources permit, it should increasingly become the practice for every clinical team in hospital, and every primary health care team outside, to have an identified social worker (or group of social workers) to whom individual cases can be referred. But where this is not yet feasible, the officer described here would also have an important role in providing a point of reference for consultants, general practitioners and other health service staff who wished to make links with social workers in particular cases.

96. The precise location of this officer seems to us to matter less than that there should be such a person who is clearly identifiable and accessible to the medical and nursing staff in the health district. *We refer to the task of this officer as being that of district co-ordinator.* It should be undertaken by someone at middle management level within the structure of the social services department. Since he will normally be concerned with support provided by a number of social services area teams in a district, he should be at least at area officer level, and possibly higher, so that he can act for all the areas. The district co-ordinator, it should be clear, is not seen as providing an exclusive channel of communication between health service and social services staff in a district. *His responsibility is to ensure a satisfactory network of contacts at working level, and to be available as a point of reference for all doctors and other health service staff in a district (whether in hospital or outside) in case of difficulty or uncertainty.* In discharging this responsibility he should be accountable to the "senior officer."

97. One advantage of giving a clear responsibility of this kind to a district co-ordinator is that he should be able to give advice on any difficulties arising from lack of correspondence between health service and local authority operational boundaries. Matching of boundaries within local authorities and AHAs was said by the Working Party on Collaboration to be a desirable aim, and we endorse this. But it has to be recognised that it will not always be possible to align boundaries, and hospital and general practice catchment areas will often spread across local authority boundaries. We think the most effective way of ironing out difficulties that may arise from this is to ensure that there is always

one officer within the organisation of the social services department to whom all medical and nursing staff in a health district know they can refer for advice on the organisation of appropriates ocial work support in particular cases.

98. There are two situations where it may be necessary to contemplate a variation of the pattern we have proposed:

(a) In an area health authority consisting of a single health district it could in theory be possible for one person to combine the roles of "senior officer" responsible for planning social work support for the AHA and of the district co-ordinator described in the preceding paragraphs. Whether or not this is possible in practice will be for local decision, but it is important not to overload a single officer with too many functions at different levels of responsibility, and we think therefore that the two functions should normally be kept separate.

(b) In London where a number of London boroughs are linked together with a single AHA, it would be open to the boroughs to agree between themselves (and in consultation with the AHA) that an officer of one borough should act as "senior officer" for the purpose of ensuring that adequate social work support is provided to the whole AHA by the boroughs concerned; otherwise (and this is more likely to be the case in practice) each borough should identify its own senior officer.

Communication and accountability at fieldwork level

99. At the basic fieldwork level the function of managerial responsibility does not arise: the function in question here is operational accountability. Much concern has been expressed over problems of "split accountability" and "divided loyalties." We think the key to resolving these lies in the emphasis we have placed on teamwork; and that different aspects of a social worker's activity must be distinguished.

100. First, *where a social worker is acting as a member of a team with doctors, nurses and possibly others, he has a professional responsibility to the team.* He is responsible to the team as a whole for:

— his professional social work advice to other members of the team on diagnosis and treatment;
— the social services aspects of the treatment decided upon (i.e. acting on the team's decisions and reporting back on the outcome);
— his operational responsibilities within the team (i.e. for such matters as attending team meetings as required or arranging a substitute).

101. But, second, *this responsibility to the team is not incompatible with accountability in other respects to the social worker's local authority department.* He will be accountable to his department for:

— the professional quality of his work;
— carrying out the responsibilities assigned to him by the department;
— observing the directions and procedures of the department.

102. The social worker's accountability to the social services department has organisational implications. Each social worker concerned with support for the health service should be a member of an operational team in the field-work section of the social services department. He should, like all other members of such teams, be accountable for his work to his team leader. In other words, we repeat the point that the social worker should always be within the normal hierarchy of responsibility in the fieldwork division of the social services department, and not located in a separate hierarchy.

103. Membership of a team in the fieldwork section does not require that the social workers concerned should be based outside hospital. Social workers based in hospital can be attached to teams outside; or where there is a large social work department in a hospital, that can constitute a team in its own right. *We wish to establish the general principle that every social worker engaged in health service support, whether in hospital or outside, should be part of the team structure of the local authority's fieldwork service, and accountable within that structure.*

104. Our analysis of functions under this general heading of "communication" can be expressed in a diagram, thus:

	Function (*a*): Managerial responsibility	Function (*b*): Operational accountability
Level (i) (AHA/LA top management)	A "senior officer"	C
Level (ii) (health district)	B "district co-ordinator"	D
Level (iii) (fieldwork)		E

The function of managerial responsibility at the top two levels runs from A to B in the first column. The operational chain of command from individual social workers to the top management of the LA department runs in the second column from E up to C. It is a matter for local decision whether the distinct operational and managerial functions at levels (i) and (ii) should be combined in one person, or discharged separately. In other words, function A could be assigned to a senior officer in the fieldwork service (C); and function B to someone at middle management level in the fieldwork service (D). However these functions are allocated, we think it necessary to distinguish them so as to avoid confusion over accountability for the two different functions. Thus the district co-ordinator at B will be responsible to the senior officer at A for managerial responsibilities within the health district. Individual fieldworkers at E will be operationally accountable within the chain of command leading up through D to C: they will not be responsible to the district co-ordinator at B (except in the case where their own senior officer in the fieldwork service is assigned the function of district co-ordinator—i.e. the roles at B and D are combined).

The organisational implications

105. Consideration of these has to start from the fact that there is no universal pattern of organisation for a social services department. The pattern adopted in a particular case varied according to the size of the authority and other factors. Terminology about different levels and areas of responsibility also varies.

106. To avoid ambiguity about the intention of our recommendations, we have sought to clarify the assumptions we are making about the organisation of local authority social services departments. We assume there are a number of key posts which occur in all structures, while other intermediate (or parallel) posts may also exist. The key posts are:

(1) Director

(2) Assistant Director (Fieldwork)

(3) Area Officer (heading one or more social work teams for a defined subdivision of the territory for which the local authority is responsible).*

There may be a Deputy Director post between 1 and 2; and in a large county there may be Divisional Directors for parts of the county, each responsible for a number of Area Officers, who may be at level 2, or interposed between 2 and 3. There may also be specialised or consultant posts at level 2 or 3.

107. In outline, the structure may be summarised thus:

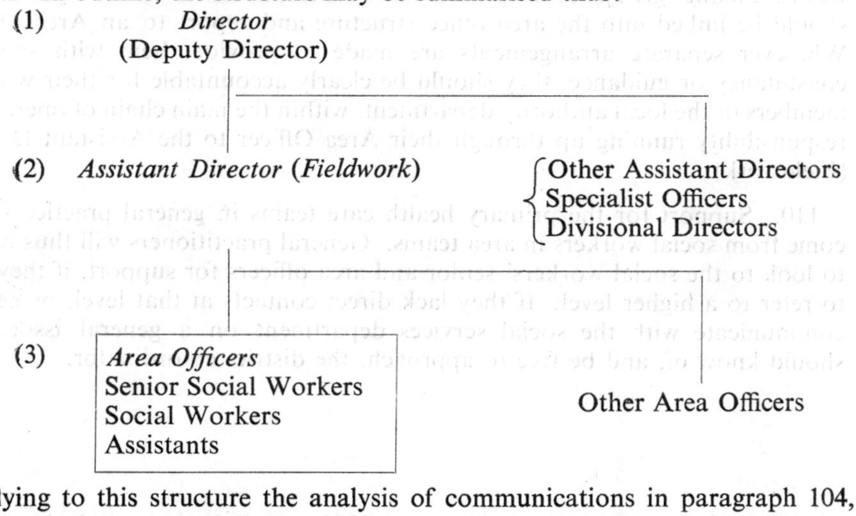

Applying to this structure the analysis of communications in paragraph 104, our conclusions are as follows. (Given the wide variety of local circumstances they are necessarily in general terms.)

* The term 'area' is used here in its local authority sense (see para (xi) of the Introduction), and is to be distinguished from a health service area for which an Area Health Authority has responsibility. The job of an 'area officer' in the local authority sense may vary considerably in weight and content.

108. For the functions of managerial responsibility the senior officer should be no lower than level (2) above, and the district co-ordinator no lower than level (3). It might appear to simplify the structure if the operational and managerial sets of functions could be combined in a single chain of command, so that the Assistant Director (Fieldwork) carried out the senior officer's managerial function as well, and one of his Area Officers carried out the district co-ordinator's function. But from our discussions it is clear that different local circumstances will require different solutions, and that some authorities will wish to assign responsibilities differently—possibly appointing special officers to carry out the managerial functions. We do not therefore attempt to recommend this—or any other arrangement—as a standard solution.

109. All social workers based in hospitals should be integrated into the area structure at level (3). The hospital departments in which they work at present contain, according to their size, officers at these levels:

Principal 2
Principal 1
Senior Social Worker
Social Worker
Assistant

A large hospital department, with a Principal in charge, can best be fitted in by becoming a team in its own right, the Principal broadly equivalent in the organisation to an Area Officer, and reporting to the Assistant Director (Fieldwork). Smaller groups of hospital social workers, at senior or basic grade level, should be linked into the area office structure and report to an Area Officer. Whatever separate arrangements are made to provide them with specialist consultancy or guidance, they should be clearly accountable for their work, as members of the local authority department, within the main chain of operational responsibility running up through their Area Officer to the Assistant Director (Fieldwork).

110. Support for the primary health care teams in general practice should come from social workers in area teams. General practitioners will thus be able to look to the social workers' senior and area officers for support, if they need to refer to a higher level. If they lack direct contacts at that level, or need to communicate with the social services department on a general issue, they should know of, and be free to approach, the district co-ordinator.

CHAPTER 6

THE MANNING OF THE SERVICE

The specialised needs of health service patients

111. In the last chapter we have set out in some detail the arguments on which we base our recommendation that social work support for the health service should be provided by local authorities as an integral part of their fieldwork services. We have rejected patterns of organisation which would lead to the continuation of a separate structure, because this would make it harder for users of the health service to have access to the whole range of field, residential and day care services available from the local authority. In any case, we think that such a pattern of organisation would tend to isolate health service social work professionally at a time when there is an exceptional opportunity for the development of a more broadly based service. But in making these recommendations we do not under-value the special skills of health service social workers, and the contribution which will continue to be needed from them in future.

112. We received valuable evidence from many social workers, working in a wide range of hospitals of all kinds, about the special needs of patients of the health service and about the contribution which qualified and skilled social workers can make to meeting them. *We are impressed with the need to ensure that patients of the health service should continue to have available to them a skilled service related to the social problems of illness and disability. Where this has been available in the past, it should be maintained. Where it has not—and there are many such areas—it should be an objective of the local authority social services department to develop it.*

113. One group of social workers, in their evidence to us, gave us a statement of what they regarded as the essential nature of medical social work in a health service setting, and we reproduce part of it here:

> "Medical social work is a professional service based on the understanding of the psycho-social implications of illness and handicap. All patients who face the problems of physical helplessness, deformity and mutilation, incurable progressive illness and death, experience anxiety, fear, loss and grief. Awareness of the emotional responses to characteristic problems of illness, of handicap and of medical care, and ability to remain in close relationship no matter how distressing the situation, are the particular attributes of medical social workers. They have a responsibility to know and understand the medical situation and the implications of this for the patient and his family, the problems it presents for them and the potential stresses it brings. Medical social work can be preventive in help given with foresight of the probable social consequences for the patient and his family, including mobilising practical resources and services on his behalf. Unless medical social workers are an essential part of the reorganised health service, they cannot fulfil their role of helping sick people and their families to adjust to illness and its treatment, nor counter

the overwhelming sense for many patients and their families of isolation, depression, loss and bereavement."

114. There is a further dimension of professional skill in the field of psychiatric social work. A specialist contribution to care and concern for the mentally ill in the community stretches back to the 1890s. Social work in a psychiatric setting, whether for adults, adolescents or children, is based upon a psychodynamic awareness and understanding of the impact on the patient and his family of mental illness. This illness will take various forms, sometimes disturbing, and frequently bewildering and inexplicable to the family. Often (for example, in child psychiatry) the "referred patient" may be demonstrating a symptom of a more widespread family difficulty. The social work contribution lies in working with other disciplines in assessment and treatment of patients with mental illness and in interpreting the work of the clinical team to other social workers in the community services so that the total needs of the patient and his family for care are articulated and understood.

115. Many local authority social workers also have training and experience in dealing with illness and handicap and their social consequences. We wish to see preserved and developed within the local authority social services the sensitive understanding of the needs of patients and their families which those with such training and experience can bring to them. Partly this will be achieved through continued development in qualifying training and other forms of training (see chapter 7), but the appropriate deployment of staff with the relevant skills and experience will also have a part to play. It was for this reason, for example, that we recommended that the "senior officer" who is to be responsible for organising social work for the health service in each area should, wherever possible, have a background of experience in working with the health service. Equally, *it will be necessary to ensure by the appropriate deployment of social workers in each locality that all available experience and knowledge is placed at the disposal of the health service, and that other social workers, at present without experience of this work, should be enabled to learn at first hand, and under skilled professional supervision and guidance, the particular needs of health service patients and their families.* The "district co-ordinator" recommended in Chapter 5 will have an important part to play in the health service district in bringing about the necessary working contacts.

116. In many areas the skilled groups of health service social workers who are already working in hospitals will provide a nucleus for further development. Other areas—perhaps a majority—will not be so fortunate in their existing resources. *Directors of Social Services now have a new responsibility in this field, and we think they should make it an early task to consult with those experienced health service social workers available to them and consider how their skills may be made available to the health service (including primary health care teams) in the most effective way.* We think, too, that *local authorities should attempt at an early date to assess the total resources needed to provide adequate social work for the health service within their area; to work out how best to deploy existing resources; and to begin to plan to meet the full need in the long term.* In this the senior staff of the social services department will need to work closely

with the community physicians and nursing staff of the AHA. *The sub-committee of the Joint Consultative Committee concerned with social work in the health service (recommended by the Working Party on Collaboration in paragraph 5.26 of its first report) will wish to keep under careful review the process of assessment and planning and, through the Joint Consultative Committee, advise its parent authorities on progress.*

117. In the evidence given to us there has been a great deal of emphasis on the importance of continuity of care. We think that there are a number of different aspects of continuity which need to be identified.

(i) Continuity of service is the base from which social services departments organise all their work, so that the needs of individual families are seen as a whole and delivery of the necessary services is carried out in an integrated rather than a piecemeal fashion.

(ii) Teamwork is essential if this is to be achieved; it is not realistic, and not always desirable, to assume that one worker can meet the varied needs at all times of one individual or family. Continuity of care for the family therefore demands a system which will ensure that there is a team responsibility to co-ordinate any action and prevent either overlap or gaps in the help offered.

(iii) Continuity between care in hospital and care in the community is of the greatest importance. Some patients may already have a helpful relationship with a local authority social worker who is not a member of the clinical team—or with a probation officer who is not a member of the social services department at all. We think it important that any system of support should take account of this and allow for patients to be looked after by the social workers they already know, when this will be of most benefit to them.

(iv) Continuity in membership of a team is also important. As we have said in an earlier chapter, a team will not work efficiently if its members are constantly changing. We are aware of the problems which arise when staff are in short supply and a certain amount of movement is inevitable. Nevertheless, continuity of care for clients depends on stability in the composition of the various teams in health and social services, and in the arrangements for linking them.

(v) Finally continuity of work for any individual team worker is important for job satisfaction and for the development of professional skill, which will not be attained without reasonably long periods of practice in one setting.

Continuity in all these dimensions cannot be regulated by ground-rules about length of service in particular settings. But its attainment should be a conscious aim of social services departments, in planning the development both of services and of careers. One implication is that specialisation in health service social work will continue to be needed as one means to securing continuity in some of its aspects.

Specialisation in health service social work

118. Many health service social workers wish to remain in this field of work, and this fact has been recognised by section 18(5) of the National Health Service Reorganisation Act 1973, which has provided that health service social workers transferred to local authority service shall not be required to perform duties otherwise than at or in connection with a hospital unless they have consented to do so. This was a transitional provision, only affecting those in hospital posts at the date of transfer. In fact we would expect that many hospital social workers covered by this provision will want to take advantage of the wider opportunities for gathering experience in other settings that are now open to them as a result of the transfer, and which they will need to acquire if they are to progress to the highest posts in the service. Similarly, newly qualified social workers entering the service in future are likely to regard hospitals as one only of the settings in which they will wish to practise. Nevertheless, we think it important that local authorities should seek to accommodate within social services departments the different preferences of individual social workers, so far as is consistent with the needs of the service. To quote from one statement sent to us, "most hospital social workers are in hospital because they choose to be; . . . it is essential that we should not do anything which will cause us to lose the skills and experiences of a number of committed and professional workers." *We think it should continue to be possible for those whose chief inclination and motivation is towards work in a hospital setting to pursue specialisation in that setting.*

119. As we have explained in Chapter 5, there is a range of tasks which call for the basing of social workers in hospital, and the opportunities for work in this setting should be no less in future than they have been in the past. Although advancement to the highest levels of social services departments will inevitably depend upon the acquisition of a wide range of experience in as many aspects of the work of a department as possible, the social worker who wishes to confine himself to hospital-based work will still have opportunities for advancement in many local authorities within his chosen specialism—for example to a specialist post at senior management level. But the opportunities for such a social worker to widen his experience are likely to be considerably increased in other ways by the transfer of responsibility to local authorities. In the long run the transfer is bound to result in new models of practice and to affect the way in which social work is practised, even by those remaining in hospital. It is of the essence of the change that the nature of the task should be altered to a degree by the new focus it will be given as part of a wider social work operation. We hope, therefore, that those involved in the change, even where they exercise their right to remain in hospital duties, will be receptive to the new opportunities which the system offers.

The benefit to social services departments

120. We have placed much emphasis in the report on the need to integrate social work in the health service with the rest of the local authority social services, with a view to the benefits that this may be expected to bring to the health service in the longer run. Equally, however, we wish to stress the benefits

which the change will bring to the rest of the local authority services. *The special skills and experience of social workers with health service experience will be of value in a number of other settings—for example, in residential care, and in the management of long-term disability. We think that much may be achieved by a carefully devised policy of cross-posting of staff between hospitals and other appropriate parts of the local authority social services.* We endorse the attitude expressed in a statement sent to us by one group of hospital social workers:

> "The reorganisation of the health service affords a major challenge to all professions working within its framework. As social workers in the health service, we wish to preserve, share and develop the knowledge and experience which we have gained from working within it. . . . We hope we shall be given the opportunity to share the knowledge and experience thus gained to a yet greater degree with our colleagues in all fields of social work."

121. We also wish to commend to the attention of local authorities certain practices which have grown up in hospital social work departments which may be of value in a wider application. Many hospitals make extensive use of part-time social workers who are unable, for reasons of family commitments, to work full-time and might therefore find it difficult, as things are at present, to obtain local authority employment. These part-time workers are a resource which cannot be dispensed with; and their transfer to local authority employment means that some local authorities will for the first time be employing part-time social workers—a practice previously followed in a minority only of social services departments because of the different patterns of working demanded by local authority responsibilities (e.g. for standby duties outside normal working hours). We suspect that *there may here be a considerable reservoir of talent and experience which could be tapped by local authorities more widely in future, and we recommend that consideration should be given by them to the possibility of extending their reliance on part-time social workers.* This will have significant long-term advantages if it encourages married women with social work skills to "keep in touch" through the period when they are caring for their young families.

122. *We also wish to commend to the attention of local authorities the well-established practice in hospital social work departments of senior and principal social workers carrying caseloads.* This seems to us to have great value in enabling those social workers who wish to continue in social work practice nevertheless to obtain professional advancement. An increasing number of local authorities are introducing senior professional and consultant grades to make this possible; but social workers in many local authorities are still able to obtain promotion only into administrative posts. We suggest that local authorities generally may here be able to learn something from former practice in the health service. With the recent rapid expansion of social services departments, clients are often served by unqualified or recently qualified practitioners, while officers with much professional talent and experience are preoccupied with administrative tasks at higher levels in the department. Other considerations apart, it is necessary for the training of newer staff that senior social

workers within the department should still have current practical experience on which to draw in giving guidance to trainees and younger colleagues.

Clerical and administrative support

123. We have been impressed, throughout our work, by the importance of adequate clerical and administrative support to enable health service social workers to make the best use of their skills and time. This is a need which is often recognised but which, because of chronic shortages of suitable staff in many parts of the country, is less often met in practice. Where such support, whether given by a health or a local authority, has been bad we have detected a feeling that the service not responsible might be able to provide better support for social work staff. We fear there is some unrealism about this—a case of the grass always looking greener on the other side of the fence. But whether that is true or not, we have not seen any advantage to be gained from trying to transfer supporting clerical and administrative staff in hospital social work departments to local authority employment. After careful consideration we recommend at an early stage that the transfer arrangements should not apply to these staff, who are normally part of a larger body of clerical and administrative staff in a hospital, often working only part-time for the social work department and depending on other office services common to all departments of the hospital. Where social workers are based in hospital to give a service to the hospital, it is right that the hospital should be responsible for providing all necessary accommodation and staff support.

124. We are aware of some anxiety among local authorities about this, on the ground that they will not be able to control the quality of the service they are providing if they are dependent on the health authority for supporting staff. We think this is a matter where the right solution lies in proper mutual collaboration: it will be to the interest of the hospital or the primary health care team to ensure that the social workers appointed to help it are properly supported and so enabled to function effectively. We also think that it may help, especially where small units of hospital-based social workers are concerned, to link them into the structure and services of the hospital if their clerical support is provided by the hospital's own staff. *We must emphasise, however, the importance of adequate clerical and administrative support. If a hospital or primary health care team fails to provide it, the service they can expect to receive will be impaired.* This again is among the matters which the sub-committees of Joint Consultative Committees concerned with social work for the health service will wish to keep under review.

CHAPTER 7
THE TRAINING OF SOCIAL WORKERS

125. Training calls for a separate chapter. There are important implications for training in what we have said in previous chapters, and future patterns of training can contribute much to the development of services we think desirable. We also think it important, for the development of better understanding between health and social services personnel, to include some account of the present arrangements for training social workers. By no means every social worker employed by a social services department possesses a professional qualification. That is an objective to which the service is moving, but many staff now in employment entered the service before training arrangements were developed on any scale, and the pressures on social services departments, following Seebohm, have been such that local authorities still have to fill posts, whether or not they can recruit qualified staff. In some parts of the country authorities can adhere to a policy of employing only trained social workers, but in other less favoured areas such a policy has been proved to be quite unrealistic, and a significant proportion of employed social workers may therefore be unqualified.

126. As we have already explained, the expansion of the services and now local government reorganisation, have created a more extensive hierarchy in social services departments, resulting in rapid promotion of social workers to managerial posts—particularly of those holding professional qualifications. Further, a significant majority of the qualified staff currently in employment who were trained and gained their experience in a specialised area of work, are now facing new demands on their knowledge and skills for which, in some instances, they received little or no preparation. The problems that result have created many difficulties for those responsible for the training of social workers. But they are problems resulting from political and managerial decisions—they are not problems to be laid at the door of training.

127. As a preliminary to any discussion of the training of social workers, it is necessary to make a distinction between social services provision and professional social work, both of which are provided by the local authority social services department. The social services for which they are responsible include, for example, home help services, the supply of aids for the physically handicapped, and other services which are not necessarily provided by social workers. This chapter is concerned only with the training of social workers in relation to the professional service which they are being asked to provide for the health service, and an attempt is made in the following paragraphs to set out what it is now appropriate to expect of a qualified worker.

Patterns of training: the background

128. In the past, professional education for social work has been largely service-focused; students selected their field of employment and were trained, for example, as medical social workers, or child care officers, and their qualifications were recognised by different training bodies, even though they might

share the same basic course. These qualifications in medical or psychiatric social work, child care or probation, and the certificate in social work, still stand as professional qualifications, but they have been superseded by a new unified award—the Certificate of Qualification in Social Work (CQSW). Since October 1971, the promotion and recognition of training for social work in all fields, and throughout the United Kingdom, has become the responsibility of the Central Council for Education and Training in Social Work (CCETSW), which awards the CQSW to students successfully completing a course recognised as offering professional training, regardless of their intended field of employment. This means that social workers qualifying now, both graduate and non-graduate, all hold the same basic qualification, and may be expected to have followed broadly the same basic syllabus. However, their field training and concentration of interest will vary to some extent, according to the bias of the particular course, and the field practice opportunities available in the area. The majority of qualified social workers now in employment were trained before 1972 (when the first CQSWs were awarded), and many of them are faced with new demands for which their training may have provided scant preparation; none the less, they have the basic knowledge and skills of a qualified social worker, to which further specialised knowledge may be added.

129. Social workers entering employment in any field will have to work with clients suffering physical and mental illness, or who are in some way handicapped. All courses are therefore encouraged by CCETSW to give some attention to teaching about the most commonly encountered medical and psychiatric conditions, and CCETSW has recently been studying the training needs of social workers providing services to handicapped people.*

130. Many clients known to social workers go through the experience of admission to an institution (prison, hospital or home), a period of residence, and then discharge to their own homes, or transfer to some type of community provision. Training programmes therefore, offer some teaching about institutions, their effect on residents, their families, and the staff, and they give students an opportunity to study the process of admission, residence and discharge and how the individual affected, and his family, may be helped through it.

131. In a local authority social services department a social worker has to be able to work in co-operation with other people providing services for the same client—doctors, nurses, teachers, police and court officials, and voluntary workers—and all social work students have opportunities to discuss the need for this type of co-ordinated activity, and its implication for their own work. Those who are interested in working in a setting where the primary task is not social work (e.g. in the health service, in schools, or in prisons) also have to consider the contribution which social work may make in such other services; they have to learn through field practice the particular skills of working in a team which might be led by someone from another discipline, and the problems engendered in maintaining administrative accountability inside an institution, and professional accountability outside it (as in the case of probation officers

* CCETSW—Report of Working Party on Training for Social Work with Handicapped People—(to be published in 1974).

working in the prison welfare service and, from April 1974, hospital social workers employed by local authority social services departments).

132. A qualified social worker will have studied the structure and development of the social, education, social security, employment, housing and health services, and will have some first-hand experience of the way these services affect individuals in the community. Resources, including those provided by voluntary agencies, will vary from area to area, but a qualified social worker will learn to use whatever resources are available to assist a particular family or individual. Some general knowledge of the law can be expected, although newly qualified workers are likely to need introduction to the details of professional law.*

133. Qualified social workers will have studied different methods of social work, predominantly case-work with individuals and families, but also increasingly social work with groups of clients, and work in community development and organisation. Although a newly qualified social worker cannot be expected to be equally at ease with all methods of social work, those now coming from training courses are likely to have an appreciation of the appropriate use of groups, and of community work, even though they may be more practised in providing service for families and individuals; most will have had at least a limited experience of work in an institutional setting.

134. The content of training, as outlined above, is on a developing pattern which varies to some degree on individual courses. It relates to the present and to the future, rather than to the past, for events have moved swiftly in the organisation and development of the social services, and many changes are taking place in professional education. Two points, however, emerge in particular.

135. First, the less specialised pattern of basic training now being developed increases the need for staff development programmes, ranging from orientation to specific areas of work, to opportunities for updating knowledge, and preparation for promotion to management and consultative posts. It requires a commitment on the part of employers to staff training as a continuous process, an integral part of service provision, to which resources must be allocated if standards are to be maintained and improved. The range of responsibilities which have now accrued to social services departments is such that it is quite unrealistic to imagine that standards of services can be maintained in all areas of work without significant allocation of time and resources to staff development. *We commend to the attention of the local authorities the CCETSW paper No. 1:* "*Social Work: creating opportunities for staff development*", *which makes recommendations about this aspect of staff training which should in our view find application in training staff for work with the health service.*

136. Second, we note that, although there have been a few full-time courses offering opportunity for study at post-qualification level, there has been no recognised programme of advanced training. *This too is essential if standards*

* CCETSW—Report of Study Group on Legal Studies for Social Workers.

of service are to improve, and if qualified social workers are to have the opportunities for professional advancement which they are entitled to expect. We are pleased to note the CCETSW is developing plans for advanced training in consultation with colleges, universities, local authorities, and other interests involved, some of which will no doubt be relevant for social workers interested in making a special contribution in the health field.

Social work in support of the Health Service

137. The areas of training described above are relevant and important for all social workers, including those who prefer to work either wholly or partly in an NHS setting, whether in hospital, clinic, day centre, or in general practice. Such differences in skill and knowledge as may be required of social workers in the health service are perhaps more matters of emphasis than of kind, and may partly be gained in qualifying training, and partly learned through experience and from staff development programmes. Some qualifying courses have always provided special opportunities for some students to concentrate on work in medical and psychiatric settings, and already have the necessary teaching and practice resources available in the area. These courses will no doubt continue to maintain these emphases to some degree. Others will develop a range of choices for students within the basic course, and others again may be able to provide facilities for post-qualification study for social workers in the health field. Where specialist medical services are available and are interested in contributing to the professional education of social workers, the opportunity should be taken to develop post-qualification training focused on areas of medical specialism which demand close and continuous co-operative work with a social worker.

138. In general, the skills and knowledge needed by social workers in health service settings, are also needed by other social workers, since social problems related to physical and mental illness or to the handicapped are not confined to health service settings. Particular emphasis on certain areas of learning is however important for those students who wish to work with ill or disabled people:

(i) the impact and consequences of illness and handicap for the patient and his family, both within the family and in the community;

(ii) study of the hospital as an institution, and the relationship between it and community health and social services;

(iii) the roles and responsibilities of other professional workers in the health service, including a sufficient knowledge and appreciation of their training and professional attitudes, to enable the social worker to co-operate as a member of a multi-disciplinary team.

139. Decisions about how the skills of social workers are deployed in the provision of support for the health service will have training implications. The following tasks may need to be undertaken by social workers, either as the major part of their work or as one component of it:

(i) *Long-term social work support for individual patients.* This implies becoming the patient's social worker for all purposes, and helping him over all his needs, both as a patient of the health service and in other situations, just like any other local authority social worker. Some patients may require continuous social work help for complicated or persistent social problems over a long period, while others need periodic help. Where the need for long-term work arises because the patient's condition requires continuous contact with specialist medical services, the social worker may need to have an opportunity to acquire specialist knowledge in a narrowly defined field.

(ii) *Short-term work.* One way of using qualified social work skills in the health service is to arrange the social work service in such a way that those social workers based in hospital or general practice deliberately plan to carry work with a high proportion of patients on a short-term basis . At the end of a period which is agreed with all concerned the social work is terminated, or else the patient is transferred to another social worker, or to a member of another community care profession, who will provide service for as long as it is needed. This type of short-term work requires a high degree of skill, and an acceptance by the service as a whole of the need to plan continuity of care, even though more than one social worker may be involved. But in our view it is fundamental to the development of effective social work practice in this context. Where this pattern develops, many social workers currently employed would require opportunities for learning about this particular method of working.

(iii) *Co-ordination of services.* The alternative methods of providing social work support for the health service which are discussed earlier in this report suggest an increasingly important role for at least some social workers as co-ordinators. This has always been an element in the job of a social worker, but not one on which great emphasis has been laid. If it is to develop, some in-service training provision would be helpful, taking this task as an aspect of management which requires some skills in interpreting and explaining the services required of different people, and which demands of the social worker an understanding of how to provide much of the necessary support and help indirectly, instead of face to face with the patient.

Training resources in the Health Service

140. The hospital service has for many years provided practice training facilities for social work students, and in England and Wales there are over 40 units specifically set up for the training of social workers. The organisation of these units varies considerably,* and financial support may be provided by DHSS centrally or by health authorities. Individual social workers in hospitals and clinics also supervise students as part of their professional task even where there is no formal unit, and a few students have been able to gain experience in a general practice setting. This allocation of resources to training is vitally important for social work education as a whole, and is the only way in which student social workers can obtain first hand experience of working in the health

* A study of student units will be published later in 1974 by CCETSW.

service. *The Working Party consider that the future arrangements for social work support for the health service should include the maintenance and further development of the provision of student units, and that encouragement should be given to suitable individual social workers to provide practice teaching for students in training.*

141. Many student placements at present are with teaching hospitals, and large areas of the country are without provision for placements. *We think the Department of Health and Social Security should consider, in conjunction with the CCETSW, what possibilities there may be for the wider provision of facilities for student placements in district general hospitals, psychiatric hospitals and primary health care teams.* It is essential that the standard of social work in these settings should be high, to provide for the proper training of students, and we see advantage in the development of links with universities and colleges (whether or not a joint appointment is made) because of the benefits this can bring both to the educational institutions and to local authorities.

142. The Working Party considered the position of the staff of student units employed by health authorities, and concluded that it would be right that *professional staff serving student units should transfer to local authorities in the same way as other hospital social work staff. Clerical staff should remain with the hospital, which should also be responsible for providing equipment and accommodation.* Where a supervisor has a joint appointment with a health authority and a university, the university should continue to meet their share of the total cost, but the responsibility for the health authority's share should pass to the appropriate local authority. We understand that responsibility for the units which are at present financed from central funds will remain with the DHSS. While we recognise that resources are limited, *we hope that DHSS will be able to give central support to further units in future.*

143. Qualified social workers in hospitals also make a contribution to the professional education of health service personnel and this becomes increasingly important if doctors, nurses and others are to understand how to use social work and social services for the benefit of patients. By the same token, it is important that doctors should be prepared to make a contribution to the teaching of social workers, as many of them already do.

Conclusion

144. As a conclusion to this discussion of training, we should wish to emphasise the following points:

(i) Qualifying training for social workers intending to work with ill and handicapped people will continue to be provided in the mainstream of professional education for social workers of all types. Some courses will provide greater emphasis on social work in the medical field than others, but all will include some teaching related to physical and mental illness and handicap.

(ii) Employing authorities should recognise the necessity of supporting staff development programmes to allow social workers to acquire additional knowledge about physical and mental illness and to study the role of a social worker as a member of a clinical or primary health care team. This is particularly important in the short-term, when many social workers who were trained on specialist courses are having to undertake new tasks for which they received little or no preparation in basic training. Appropriate provision should be made in the training budgets of local authorities.

(iii) In-service training will also be needed for social work assistants and other staff working under the direction of qualified workers, who have a considerable contribution to make in certain sections of the health service.

(iv) No training programmes will be successful without the co-operation of both the local authority social services departments and the health service. Only they can provide resources of personnel, accommodation and time to ensure that practice training is available, and of an adequate standard. Without it the health service will not be given the social work support which patients need.

CHAPTER 8
WORKING TOGETHER: SOME PRACTICAL SUGGESTIONS

145. The idea of better collaboration between health and local authority services has been central to the reorganisation of the health service, and as this report shows, the question of social work support for the health service has proved to raise in its acutest form the problem of inter-professional relationships which lies at the heart of collaboration. The main theme of our report has developed out of the recognition of this fact. It is that the opportunity which the transfer of responsibility offers for important new developments in social work practices in the field of health care should not be missed by clinging to the patterns of the past. Health service social work should come into the mainstream of local authority social services activities in organisational as well as professional terms; and local authorities should try to develop, from the skills which hospital social workers will bring to them, a service which will extend to new areas of the health service—and to general practice in particular—the kind of support which some parts of the National Health Service have enjoyed in the past. This will require much painstaking effort, and a willingness in both services to extend understanding to the other and to modify previous attitudes.

146. Much of this however is for the longer term. In the shorter term, local authorities will be much pre-occupied with the practical consequences of the transfer and with the need to modify their own organisation so that they will be ready to meet the demands of future developments. There will also be a number of practical steps which local authorities will need to take, in conjunction as necessary with health authorities, to ensure that there is full understanding of the new arrangements, their implications and opportunities at the various operational levels concerned. Better communication, at various levels and in various ways, is a basic requirement, both between services and between practititioners. In this chapter, therefore, we set out a few practical suggestions which may help that communication to develop.

147. *We think local authorities should give attention as quickly as possible to the provision of in-service training, both for their existing staff and their new staff, to enable them to meet the demands of reorganisation.* These are likely to be heavy, and to impose strain on all those concerned until the new arrangements are working well. *We further suggest that local authorities should invite area health authorities to join with them in providing appropriate seminars and other occasions on which health service and local authority staff who will need to work in close collaboration under the new arrangements can get to know one another and begin to see common problems from each other's perspective.* The sub-committee of the Joint Consultative Committee concerned with social work in the health service, and its supporting group of officers, should give this urgent attention.

148. We think two points need to be covered in particular:

(i) newly transferred health service social workers should be helped to understand the structure and organisation of the local authority social services department, and their own place within it;

(ii) key officers of the social services department should be helped to learn something from their new colleagues of the specific functions involved in social work practice in the health service, and the skills which need to be brought to bear.

These two aspects might, at least to begin with, be covered jointly in seminars to which the various members of staff concerned would contribute.

149. *In addition the local authority and the area health authority should jointly organise seminars in which (i) local authority members and staff acquire a basic knowledge of the new health service organisation and the needs of the health service for social work as perceived by health service staff; (ii) health service staff may similarly acquire a basic knowledge of the organisation of the local authority social services and of the contribution which these can make to the total care of patients of the health service; and (iii) the two sides may learn to understand each other's expectations in terms of the accountability and responsibility of professional staff* We commend to their attention our views on this subject in Chapter 5 of this Report.

150. We think that seminars between the health and social services should be organised at a variety of levels, and we commend the contribution being made towards the development of collaboration by the professional organisations, post-graduate medical centres, and bridging seminars being organised by a variety of academic institutions. *But we also wish to place particular stress on the importance of meetings at local level at which members of primary health care teams and hospital clinical teams can meet local authority social work staff (including former staff of the health service) with whom they will be working on a day-to-day basis.* Discussions should not only deal with the more general aspects of reorganisation, but should centre on specific subjects which will be of direct concern to the two services in the locality. Some suggestions which we offer are:

(i) the organisation of collaboration in dealing with, for example, non-accidentally injured children, or patients discharged from hospital;

(ii) the use of case conferences involving both health and local authority services;

(iii) discussions of differences in ethos between health and local authority services, as shown, for example, in different approaches to urgency in dealing with the frail elderly, and in the different and sometimes conflicting priorities of the two services.

151. It will be of great importance for seminars and meetings to take place in a planned sequence, and *we recommend that each local authority should nominate an officer to supervise the programme of training.* This officer could be the "senior officer" or the district co-ordinator of social work for the health service described in Chapter 5, the training officer in the social services department, or a separate officer appointed specifically for this task. In any event the senior officer and the specialist in community medicine concerned with

social services should jointly be involved and keep plans and progress under review.

152. The successful organisation of health service social work will be a demanding task requiring much hard work on the part of many staff of social services departments and health authorities. In addition, members of local authorities and area health authorities will have a responsibility to see that the arrangements work well, and, through the collaborative machinery of the Joint Consultative Committees, to ensure together that satisfactory arrangements are made for the provision of social work to the health service, and for the development of a joint programme of training and education. *We recommend specifically that Joint Consultative Committees should periodically review the progress of the arrangements for social work in the health service, and the central Departments should likewise at intervals review progress nationally. It will be particularly important for all concerned to ensure the spread of good practice, and we recommend that the Departments should be prepared whenever necessary to issue recommendations to local and health authorities with this in view.*

CHAPTER 9
CONCLUSIONS

153. In the course of this report we have reached a number of conclusions and recommendations which have been emphasised by italics in the text. In this chapter they are drawn together for ease of reference.

Chapter 1: The realities of collaboration

154. We take the view that there is nothing in the Seebohm Report's recommendations to imply the wholesale abandonment of specialism in social work practice. The health service will continue to need the support of social workers with specialised skills in working alongside health service staff in health settings. There must be no question of these skills being dissipated or devalued in the future. (Paras. 12, 14.)

155. We wish to emphasise the importance of personal links in achieving successful professional co-operation between health care staff and the staff of social services departments. Arrangements designed merely to establish that a social worker can be called in when necessary by impersonal communication from one system to the other are not good enough. We think it is possible and desirable to devise arrangements for doctors to communicate with the social services through a personal link well known to them and readily accessible. Similarly there should be a known channel for communication between social services and primary health care teams. (Paras. 16, 17.)

156. On the question of confidentiality we think that, for the needs of the patient to be fully understood, it is clearly right that medical and social information about him should be shared as far as necessary between those who are sharing in the task of caring for him. (Para. 18.)

157. We wish to stress the value of teamwork between the health professions and social workers as it already exists in many hospitals; the future development of social work support for the health service should build on this pattern of teamwork and seek to extend it to areas where it does not exist. (Para. 19.)

Chapter 2: Social work and the clinical team

158. We suggest that teamwork in a clinical situation means that all members of the team accept that each has a professional contribution to make in his own right; and that it is both the right and, equally, the responsibility of each member of the team to make that contribution if the patient needs it. Such a responsibility derives not from the prescription of the head of the team, but from the right of the patient to have the benefit of all the team's skills as he needs them. (Para. 33.)

159. To attain the degree of mutual respect on which teamwork must depend, some basic rules of practice can, we think, be postulated:

(i) There must be some continuing personal relationship between individuals.

(ii) Regular opportunity for face to face contact by members is essential.

(iii) Team members should report back to the team on the action they take.

(iv) It should be recognised that priorities will often be differently assessed by different members of the team.

(v) The social worker attached to a team should not necessarily be expected to carry all responsibility for the social work follow-up of every case. (Paras. 37-42.)

Chapter 3: Social work and primary health care

160. We make a strong plea that experimentation in the field of social work and primary health care should receive urgent consideration by the professions and by the health and local authorities. (Para. 44.)

161. We hope that all new health centres will be designed to include accommodation for the use of social workers. (Para. 45.)

162. The family doctor has an interest in being informed whenever patients on his list are receiving help from a social services department. Conversely, further reference by a family doctor to a social worker may not only be appropriate to the patient's immediate needs, but may prevent the development of more complex situations of stress and breakdown in health. (Paras- 47, 48.)

163. We think that there are opportunities in primary health care teams, as in hospital clinical teams, for the practice of complementary kinds and levels of expertise by members of the team which will lead to a more comprehensive service to their clients. (Para. 49.)

164. Generally, we see development of support for general practice as a priority for the future, since it presents a major opportunity for significant improvement in methods of health and social care. (Para. 53.)

Chapter 5: Management and organisation

165. The overriding objective should be to devise organisational arrangements which promote the integration of social work in support of general practice and hospitals with the full range of services provided by the local authority social services department. The aim should be continuity of care wherever the needs of the individual or the family indicate this: and the organisational structure should aim at integrating social work support for patients receiving health care within the fieldwork services of the department, rather than preserving them in a separate compartment. (Para. 78.)

166. A second main objective should be to promote teamwork between doctors, nurses and social workers. (Para. 79.)

Support for general practice

167. In order to integrate social workers working with primary health care teams into the main structure of the local authority department, they should be members of local authority area teams. (Paras. 80, 110.)

168. Because general practitioners' patients do not come from defined catchment areas, the arrangements should be flexible enough to allow attached social workers to care for patients coming from outside their own social services areas where appropriate. (Para. 80.)

Support for hospitals

169. The needs of patients in particular types of hospital provision justify the basing of social workers in hospital. Paragraph 82 suggests the types of unit and specialty where we consider that social workers should be so based; and paragraph 83 sets out a number of other purposes for which social workers may also need to be based in hospital.

170. We think that a comprehensive pattern of social work support for hospitals should develop—as staff resources permit—on the lines of providing both hospital and community based social workers in support of hospital teams. But whether social workers are based inside or outside hospital, working arrangements must permit those based in hospital to follow cases into the community, and those based outside to follow cases into hospital, wherever this is appropriate and best serves the patient's needs. (Para. 85.)

Linking the hospital and community care teams

171. Joint Consultative Committees should particularly concern themselves with the problem of linking the hospital and community care teams, to ensure that a pattern of arrangements appropriate to local circumstances is devised. They have been asked to set up special sub-committees to deal with social work support for the health service, and these should make a point of ensuring that officers of the two services work out suitable local arrangements. (Para. 86.)

Communication

172. We regard good communication between health and social services as the single most important feature for bringing the two services into partnership. (Para. 89.)

173. We recommend that the local authority's "senior officer" (as proposed by the Working Party on Collaboration) should be appointed near the top of the social services department to be responsible for arranging social work support for the health service, for discussion with the area health authority, and for the forward planning of services relating to the health service. Wherever possible, he should be professionally qualified in social work with an understanding of casework requirements, and should have some experience of the provision of social work in a health service context and knowledge of the particular problems and needs of the health service. (Para. 94.)

174. We also identify a function of managerial responsibility in respect of social work support for the health service to be carried out in health districts. There is a need for a professionally skilled officer of appropriate seniority to act as a central point of reference in each health district for the management of social work activity in support of the health district. We refer to the task of this officer as being that of district co-ordinator. His responsibility is to ensure a satisfactory network of contacts at working level, and to be available as a point of reference for all doctors and other health service staff in a district (whether in hospital or outside) in case of difficulty or uncertainty. (Paras. 95-97.)

Communication and accountability at fieldwork level

175. Much concern has been expressed to us over problems of "split

accountability" and "divided loyalties" at the fieldwork level. We think however that the key to resolving these lies in the emphasis which we have placed on teamwork; and that different aspects of a social worker's activity must be distinguished. (Para. 99.)

176. Where a social worker is acting as a member of a team with doctors, nurses and possibly others, he has a professional responsibility to the team. But this responsibility to the team is not incompatible with accountability in other respects to the social worker's local authority department. (Paras. 100, 101.)

177. We wish to establish the general principle that every social worker engaged in health service support, whether in hospital or outside, should be part of the team structure of the local authority's fieldwork service, and accountable within that structure. (Para. 103.) In paragraphs 105-110 we suggest what the organisational implications of this general principle are, within the typical structure of a social services department.

Chapter 6: The manning of the service

178. We are impressed with the need to ensure that patients of the health service should continue to have available to them a skilled service related to the social problems of illness and disability. Where this has been available in the past, it should be maintained. Where it has not—and there are many such areas—it should be an objective of the local authority social services departments to develop it. (Para. 112.)

179. It will be necessary to ensure by the appropriate deployment of social workers in each locality that all available experience and knowledge is placed at the disposal of the health service, and that other social workers, at present without experience of this work, should be enabled to learn at first hand, and under skilled professional supervision and guidance, the particular needs of health service patients and their families. (Para. 115.)

180. Directors of Social Services should make it an early task to consult with those experienced health service social workers available to them, and consider how their skills may be made available to the health service (including primary health care teams) in the most effective way. Local authorities should attempt at an early date to assess the total resources needed to provide adequate social work for the health service within their area; to work out how best to deploy existing resources; and to begin to plan to meet the full need in the long-term. The sub-committee of the Joint Consultative Committee concerned with social work in the health service will wish to keep under careful review the process of assessment and planning and, through the Joint Consultative Committee, advise its parent authorities on progress. (Para 116).

181. Paragraph 117 analyses a number of different aspects of continuity in the care of clients. We take the view that continuity in all these dimensions cannot be regulated by ground-rules about length of service in particular settings. But its attainment should be a conscious aim of social services departments, in planning the development both of services and of careers.

182. We think it should continue to be possible for those whose chief inclination and motivation is towards work in a hospital setting to pursue specialisation in that setting. (Para. 118.)

183. The special skills and experience of social workers with health service experience will be of value in a number of other settings, for example, in residential care, and the management of long-term disability. We think that much may be achieved by a carefully devised policy of cross-posting of staff between hospitals and other appropriate parts of the local authority social services. (Para. 120.)

184. We are impressed with the value to hospitals of the services of part-time social workers, and note that their transfer to local authority employment means that some local authorities will for the first time be employing part-time social workers. We suspect that there may be a considerable reservoir of talented and experienced social workers, unable for personal reasons to work full-time but prepared to work part-time, which could be tapped by local authorities more widely in future, and we recommend that consideration should be given by them to the possibility of extending their reliance on part-time social workers. (Para. 121.)

185. We also wish to commend to the attention of local authorities the well-established practice in hospital social work departments of senior and principal social workers carrying caseloads. (Para. 122.)

186. We emphasise the importance of adequate clerical and administrative support. If a hospital or primary health care team fails to provide it, the service they can expect to receive will be impaired. (Para. 124).

Chapter 7: The training of social workers

187. We commend to the attention of local authorities Paper No. 1 of the Central Council for Education and Training in Social Work: "Social Work: Creating opportunities for staff development", which makes recommendations about this aspect of staff training which should in our view find application in training staff for work with the health service. (Para. 135.)

188. Training for social workers at advanced level is also essential if standards of service are to improve, and if qualified social workers are to have the opportunities for professional advancement which they are entitled to expect. (Para. 136.)

189. We consider that the future arrangements for social work support for the health service should include the maintenance and further development of the provision of student units, and that encouragement should be given to suitable individual social workers to provide practice teaching for students in training. (Para. 140.)

190. We think that the Department of Health and Social Security should consider, in conjunction with the Central Council for Education and Training in Social Work, what possibilities there may be for the wider provision of facilities for student placements in general hospitals, psychiatric hospitals and primary health care teams. (Para. 141.)

191. Professional staff serving student units should transfer to local authorities in the same way as other hospital social work staff. Clerical staff should remain with the hospital, which should also be responsible for providing equipment and accommodation. (Para. 142.)

192. We hope that DHSS will be able to give central support to further student units in future. (Para. 142.)

Chapter 8: Working together: some practical suggestions

193. We think that local authorities should give attention as quickly as possible after 1 April 1974 to the provision of in-service training, both for their existing staff and their new staff, to enable them to meet the demands of reorganisation. We further suggest that local authorities should invite area health authorities to join with them in providing appropriate seminars and other occasions on which health service and local authority staff, who will need to work in close collaboration under the new arrangements, can get to know one another and begin to see common problems from each other's perspective. (Para. 147.)

194. In addition, the local authority and the area health authority should jointly organise seminars in which (i) local authority members and staff may acquire a basic knowledge of the new health service organisation and the need of the health service for social work as perceived by health service staff; (ii) health authority members and health service staff may similarly acquire a basic knowledge of the organisation of the local authority social services and of the contribution which these can make to the total care of patients of the health service; and (iii) the two sides may learn to understand each other's expectations in terms of the accountability and responsibility of professional staff. (Para. 149.)

195. We also wish to place particular stress on the importance of meetings at local level at which members of primary health care teams and hospital clinical teams can meet local authority social work staff (including former staff of the health service) with whom they will be working on a day-to-day basis. (Para. 150.)

196. We recommend that each local authority should nominate an officer to supervise the programme of seminars and meetings which we have recommended. (Para. 151.)

197. We recommend that Joint Consultative Committees should periodically review the progress of the arrangements for social work in the health service, and the central Departments should likewise at intervals review progress nationally. It will be particularly important for all concerned to ensure the spread of good practice, and we recommend that the Departments should be prepared whenever necessary to issue recommendations to local and health authorities with this in view. (Para. 152.)

Printed in England for Her Majesty's Stationery Office by
McCorquodale Printers Ltd., London
HM 6898 Dd. 502796 K.32 8/74 McC 3309

